PENGUI

Blue Above the Chimneys

Christine Marion Fraser was the author of over twenty bestselling books, both fiction and non-fiction, and was most famous for her Rhanna series. In total, her books have sold well over three and half million copies. She died in 2002.

Blue Above the Chimneys

CHRISTINE MARION FRASER

PENGUIN BOOKS

PENGUIN BOOKS

Published by the Penguin Group
Penguin Books Ltd, 80 Strand, London WC2R 0RL, England
Penguin Group (USA) Inc., 375 Hudson Street, New York, New York 10014, USA
Penguin Group (Canada), 90 Eglinton Avenue East, Suite 700, Toronto, Ontario,
Canada M4P 2Y3 (a division of Pearson Penguin Canada Inc.)
Penguin Ireland, 25 St Stephen's Green, Dublin 2, Ireland (a division of Penguin Books Ltd)
Penguin Group (Australia), 250 Camberwell Road, Camberwell, Victoria 3124, Australia
(a division of Pearson Australia Group Pty Ltd)
Penguin Books India Pvt Ltd, 11 Community Centre, Panchsheel Park,
New Delhi – 110 017, India
Penguin Group (NZ), 67 Apollo Drive, Rosedale, Auckland 0632, New Zealand
(a division of Pearson New Zealand Ltd)
Penguin Books (South Africa) (Pty) Ltd, 24 Sturdee Avenue, Rosebank, Johannesburg 2196,
South Africa

Penguin Books Ltd, Registered Offices: 80 Strand, London WC2R 0RL, England

www.penguin.com

First published by Hutchinson & Co. Ltd 1980
Published in Fontana Paperbacks 1985
Published in Penguin Books 2012
001

Set in 12.75/15pt Garamond MT Std
Typeset by Jouve (UK), Milton Keynes
Printed in England by Clays Ltd, St Ives plc

ISBN: 978–140–592794–9

www.greenpenguin.co.uk

MIX
Paper from responsible sources
FSC™ C018179
www.fsc.org

Penguin Books is committed to a sustainable future for our business, our readers and our planet. This book is made from Forest Stewardship Council™ certified paper.

To the memory of Mam and Da

A Born Tomboy

It was high summer, the evenings were long and warm. Tall chimney stacks, row upon row of them, prodded into misty skies. The backcourts were alive with sun-tanned, grimy children. There was no place in our horizons to see the setting of the sun so we had no idea of the passage of time.

The Second World War was two years in the past. In the latter part of its duration I had arrived into the world. It was March. The cold breath of winter still blew on the window panes but our kitchen was warm enough to keep out the chilly winds. The fire crackled in the hearth. All was silent but for Mam's gasping sobs as I pushed my way out of the warm shell of her womb. So I was born, in a humble kitchen of a tenement in the Govan district of Glasgow, my first lusty cries shattering the silence. Mam's arms waited to hold me in the loving embrace that had cradled my four brothers and three sisters before me.

Early recollections are hard to pin down. There is no clear idea of the sequence of things. When you first spoke and walked. The indignity of being enthroned on a hard-rimmed container when hitherto you had been allowed to let go as you pleased into a nice warm nappy. Perhaps a tiny infant is so busy absorbing all that goes on in its immediate world there are no possible spaces left for memories. Like everyone else I slept, ate, soiled myself and remembered none of it. Later I loved listening to Mam telling me what I was like in those early days and I conjured a cosy picture of myself, tiny, helpless, lovable, not at all like the little warrior I became when infancy turned to young childhood. This is when my memories materialize and where my story must really begin, my story of green acres of happiness and black depths of despair mingling and weaving into my life among the dusty grey tenements of Govan.

'Come and buy! Come and buy! Oor wee shop is o-pen!' chanted my brother, Alec, peeping above two old tea chests on which were arrayed a number of mangled toys.

Although the clamour of life filled the June night I was aware of my father's presence even before I looked up and saw his iron-grey head sticking out from our kitchen window one flight up, his eagle eyes raking through the tumbling throng at the boxes in a search for his brood of four.

Sidling backwards along the dusty walls for a few yards I then scurried for the shelter of the close and tried to attract Alec's attention. But his senses were no match for mine. He hadn't spotted Da and was absorbed in fighting off a cheeky urchin who was determined to help himself to the decrepit goods in our shop.

'Alec! Chris!' Da's roar soared through space. 'Upstairs this minute! If ye see Kirsty and Ian send them up as well . . .' Aggression flooded my being at the idea of having to abandon the 'shop'. One snot-nosed boy had been on the point of purchasing a dilapidated pencil case. The sticky penny had been in his hand; now he would have the whole night to reconsider the deal.

'Da's calling,' I shouted to Kirsty, who was in deep conversation with her best friend, a girl who hailed from the landing above ours. The higher the landings, the better the standard of living seemed to be. Morag's house was another world, full of cosy carpets and comfortable furniture. She had a young brother my age, who didn't think it the least unusual to own a boxful of toy cars. It was an awesome treat to be invited to his landing to play with his toys and peek covertly into his plush carpeted lobby.

Kirsty came slowly, her four years' seniority giving her a restrained dignity. She looked disdainfully at Alec hopping on the stairs, but dropped her cool long enough to call lustily, 'O-pen!' It was a password that we all used when ascending the stairs, in the hope that the door would magically open before we reached it. But it wasn't magic which opened it now, it was Da, wrenching it back on its hinges. 'I hear ye!' he said testily. 'I've a good mind to lock the lot of ye outside! It's past ten o'clock!'

'We didn't know, Da,' said Kirsty as we piled into

the dark lobby and into the kitchen. It was like an oven after the heat of the day, the sashes thrown wide to catch the cool night air. The gas mantles hadn't yet been lit, and dark blobs of furniture merged into the dimness. It was a room of reasonable size, but the faded pink distemper on the walls made it look smaller. Broad shelves ran the length of one wall. Rows of delft cups hung on hooks. Beside them hung one special cup made of china and painted with red roses. It was Mam's cup, a small reminder of days when she had known better things.

A varnished brown dresser stood squarely at the window, its scratched surface almost hidden by a jumble of brushes, combs and knick-knacks. To the right of the dresser was the door to the scullery. Mam was at the cooker, making the supper. She had already laid the table, an oblong monstrosity with bulging legs, scrubbed white, protected from stains by layers of newspaper. The huge kitchen range gleamed dully in the half-light. Each Sunday Kirsty polished it with black lead, giving it a satin-smooth surface that was lovely to touch.

On either side of the kitchen door the dark caverns of double-bed recesses were brightened by woollen bedspreads crocheted by Mam.

Muted sounds of life came from the backcourts, filtering in through the jungle of marigolds and Tom Thumbs in Da's window box.

'Right, everybody,' called Mam from the scullery,

'the cocoa's ready.' She looked round the door. 'Where's Ian?'

'He wasn't with us,' said Alec in his quiet nervous voice.

'I'll skin him when he gets in!' threatened Da, lowering himself into one of two chairs in the room. It was a rickety little chair, dark with varnish, faded brocade padding the seat, the open-weave raffia of the upright backrest yellow with age. Although it was an ugly chair, it was considerably more comfortable than the other which was hard and straight, with a cushion tied to the seat to soften the unyielding contours. This was Mam's chair. She never exploited Da's position as head of the house by sitting in his chair.

She emerged from the scullery bearing a tray heavy with mugs of steaming cocoa and a plate piled high with doorsteps of bread and jam. She was a small-boned woman with a sensitive face, green eyes and a thick head of naturally waving auburn hair. An Aberdonian, she had the couthy sense of humour common to the warm-hearted folk of the north-east coast, and she was gifted with the ability to make people laugh.

Normally slim, she now moved with the heavy, awkward gait of pregnancy, her time to give birth imminent. I had seen the change gradually and thought nothing of it, but Kirsty was more knowing and rushed to take the tray.

'That's the door,' I piped, breathless from gulping hot, sweet cocoa.

'Go and open it, Kirsty,' instructed Mam.

Alec and I looked at each other, hugging ourselves in devilish anticipation of the scene we knew would follow that hurried knock. Ten-year-old Ian came in, tumbled and dishevelled, one sock up, the other lying in crumpled folds at his ankle, large smears of dust all over his jersey.

'Where the hell have *you* been?' asked Da, his voice ominously quiet.

'Just playing,' sniffed Ian, a touch of defiance in his tones.

'Jist playin', eh?' came Da's inevitable roar. He got up and grabbed Ian by the scruff of the neck. 'Look at ye! I've seen a cleaner tramp! Get into that scullery, wash yourself, then get out here and clean all the shoes!'

'But it's not my turn,' whimpered Ian, his defiance waning under Da's tyranny.

'*Turn!* I'll turn ye! Another word and I'll skin yer hide!'

The rest of us sat with piously prim faces, glad to be escaping the brunt of Da's black mood. He had been drinking, just enough to turn him into a being to be avoided.

'Don't hit him, John,' pleaded Mam wearily.

'Hit him! I'll knock his bloody heid off!' was Da's grim rejoinder. He glowered at everyone, then retired once more to his chair which afforded a grandstand view of all that went on in the tiny scullery. Ian ran cold water into a basin in the sink, stripped to the waist and lathered soap over his goose-pimpled flesh.

'Don't forget yer neck,' warned Da, before turning his attention to the rest of us. We had finished supper and were going through the nightly performance of stripping off to be washed. Kirsty scrubbed us, her green eyes intent on searching out the usual patches of hidden dirt. Under Da's watchful gaze she was more thorough than usual, but when we lined up for his inspection he merely grunted to indicate his approval.

Ian squatted on the floor, surrounded by dusty shoes, his face red with effort as he spat, rubbed and brushed. He threw an ugly look at Da's back. It had been Alec's turn for the shoes and Ian made his displeasure quite plain with his scowls.

'Put some elbow grease into it!' commanded Da sharply. Ian polished harder. Da sucked at his pipe. Great billows of smoke invaded the stuffy atmosphere and for a time peace reigned. Da shredded tobacco with a stained knife, the pipe clenched between his teeth, removed only when he felt the urge to hurl his spit into the low-burning fire.

Kirsty was kneeling before Mam, her loosened pigtails hanging in crinkled loops around her face. It was 'bone-comb night', a twice-weekly performance which Kirsty dreaded in case she had carried home lice from school. Fumes from the bowl of disinfectant mingled with the smoke from Da's pipe. The fine-tooth comb relentlessly tugged into Kirsty's shining russet mop and she squirmed.

'Aha!' exclaimed Mam, peering with interest at the comb. Kirsty's eyes were bright with tears which she didn't dare spill in front of Da. 'Only one,' said Mam in slightly disappointed tones. 'Right, your turn, Chris.'

The fine teeth of the comb scratched into my scalp. Having none of Kirsty's reserve, I patiently allowed Mam to delve through my thick tresses, my attention wickedly taken up by the sight of Da relentlessly cropping Ian's hair. Ian was scowling ferociously while his brown hair cascaded round his shoulders in jagged heaps.

'There ye are!' Da blew the loose hairs away from Ian's neck and whipped the towel round Alec's shoulders. He was nervous during the operation and sniffed continually while his head was pushed roughly this way and that.

Da stood back to survey his handiwork with pride. 'There ye are, right doon tae the wid!' he declared with sadistic fervour. 'Any beasts lodgin' there will just die of pneumonia!'

He sniggered delightedly at his own joke, but the boys threw black looks at their self-appointed hairdresser.

It was time to troop through to bed. Da's meagre wage from the Govan shipyards didn't allow for the luxury of fancy pyjamas, so we wore a motley collection of worn knickers and old vests, kept specially for nightwear. Alec and I were too young to care very much but Kirsty had grown dissatisfied with such an indignity and Ian was positively disgusted at having to wear girls' knickers now that he had reached the manly age of ten.

'Goodnight, Mam,' we chorused, love lighting our faces.

She patted our heads and said, 'Goodnight, my wee lamb,' to each of us as we filed past her.

'Goodnight, Da,' we said with less enthusiasm.

'Goodnight,' he said gruffly. 'I'll be through later so mind . . . none o' yer shenanigans.'

'Shenanigans, shenanigans,' I chanted softly, loving the sound of the huge word Da used when referring to nonsense.

He looked at me sharply. 'What are ye whisperin' about, Chris?' he asked, suspicion edging his tones.

'Nothing, Da,' I answered innocently. 'I was just singing to myself.'

We piled into the lobby, an L-shaped cavern, our spirits rising now that we were out of Da's sight.

'You'll do the shoes twice now,' Ian growled at Alec, his bravado surfacing once more.

'No, I won't, I'll tell Da on you,' said Alec, his words falling over each other quickly. He was two years older than I but small and slight for his age. We went everywhere together. He followed me in everything and I was always quick to defend him with my ready hands and quick tongue. Rising to his defence at Ian's words,

I said righteously, 'You shouldn't have come in so late. Da was quite right to make you do the shoes.'

'Aw, shut up!' he growled and climbed into the big double bed with brass ends and brass knobs that could be unscrewed. We each had a knob, inside which were stored small personal treasures. Woe betide anyone who violated the privacy of the others! We got into the bed after Ian, Kirsty and I at the top, Alec beside Ian at the bottom.

The spacious room still retained the light of the long June evening. We were all a little scared in the room, especially in the thick, black nights of winter. Kirsty and Ian scoffed when Alec and I voiced our fears, but I sensed in them the same apprehensions. It wasn't really so much the room that instilled fear in us, it was the pictures that adorned the walls. Paintings of ancestors in heavy gilt frames that caught the dust, portraits of people belonging to a bygone era. Big-busted women stared seriously from eyes hauntingly sad. Abundant quantities of hair were swept into unnatural bouffancy above high, smooth foreheads; swanlike necks were adorned with cameos on velvet bands. Men sported twirled moustaches, chains dangled from pocket watches to rest on tweed waistcoats, peculiar eyes stared at you with unyielding accusation.

One picture had a particularly eerie quality. It was a portrait of a young man, dark, handsome, his thumbs hooked cockily into the lapels of his waistcoat, his piercing eyes looking straight into the room, seeking you out no matter how much you tried to evade them. He hung opposite our bed, directly in line with my vision. The darker the room, the more intense his gaze. When he could be seen no more in the gloom, the fear of him became worse; you knew the eyes were there, watching you in the dark. Sometimes I could hardly contain my rising terror and sought refuge under the blankets, feeling it was far better to suffocate than have my wits scared out of me. Da would not allow the pictures to be taken down. He told Mam we weren't to be turned into cissies. 'Never give in to yer fears' was his favourite motto. One made up by himself, of course!

We lay in the hot, sticky bed, kicking fiercely at straying feet and humping bottoms. My ears were straining, listening tensely. Sometimes when Da had too much to drink he and Mam argued. If he was really drunk he occasionally hit her. We were always on the alert, ready to rush through and protect Mam with all the strength of our childish passions. But all was quiet tonight and my breathing became easier. I was inclined to hold the air in my lungs so that the sound of it escaping wouldn't detract from my listening senses, but after a while the sound of my heart in my ears made me let go of my breath in a drawn-out whoosh.

'Goodnight, Mam!' I shouted and the others took up the cry.

'Goodnight, lambs!' the reassuring voice filtered softly through the wall.

'We'll see you in the morning,' cried Kirsty gently.

One of us said this every night. Everything would always be all right as long as she was there in the morning.

Several minutes later I shouted again, 'Goodnight, Mam.'

'Shut up,' grunted Ian, and Kirsty added, 'Da will skelp your lugs if you don't be quiet.'

'Goodnight, Chris,' the muted tones filtered comfortingly through the wall, giving me the courage to kick Ian who immediately kicked Kirsty, the only one he thought would dare do such a thing to him.

Alec began sniffing, which meant he was getting ready to cry. 'You hurt my ankle,' he accused no one in particular.

'Cry baby,' sneered Ian. 'I'll kick your wullie off in a minute!'

It was the ultimate threat. Ian had very long toenails. Alec abruptly ceased to sniff.

Some time later Da came creeping through on his nightly round. Closing my eyes quickly, I hid behind the little barrier of blanket I had made in order to escape the prying eyes of the picture. Da made no sound. He had a habit of slipping into the room, waiting a few moments then clicking the door shut in an effort to trick us into thinking he had departed. From time to time he varied the procedure, but we had all grown wise to his cunning. He didn't have to use his little ruses with me. I knew the feel of his strong, dominant presence.

'Get to sleep the lot o' ye,' he muttered, just in case the peaceful snoring from the bed was only a front and we would start our 'shenanigans' the second his back was turned. I emitted a very realistic snore. He sniffed and the door closed softly behind him.

My eyes were growing heavy when I heard the key turn in the outside door, admitting the last member of the family into the house. It was Mary, our seventeen-year-old half-sister, the only child from Mam's first marriage still living at home. We all loved her. She was our protector from childhood fears, a romantic figure in our young lives. Forcing my eyes to stay open, I waited for her to come through. She came on tip-toe, going straight to the single bed recess in the wall.

'Goodnight, Mary,' I whispered.

'You not asleep yet?' she asked in her cheery voice.

'Nearly, I was waiting for you. Where were you?'

'At the pictures.'

'On your own?' I asked, knowing the answer full well.

'No, with a boy . . . but you're too wee to ask such questions.' She held out her hand. 'Here – I saved you all a bit of chocolate.'

I took the tit-bit eagerly. 'Can I eat it now?'

'Ay, but don't tell Da or I'll get it on the ear for giving you sweeties in bed.'

I savoured the chocolate, feeling grown up and special, the youngest of the family yet still awake and talking to Mary.

'Go to sleep now,' she ordered. 'I was through seeing Mam for a minute and she's not too well. We'll all have an early rise in the morning.'

Immediately my pulses raced with dread. 'What's wrong with Mam?'

Mary paused, then said softly, 'You're too wee to understand, Chris.'

I frowned in the darkness. 'No, I'm not,' I declared stoutly. 'Mam's having a baby soon. I know about babies. They grow in your belly. Did you know that, Mary?'

She chuckled. 'Ay, now that you've told me. It's getting them out of your belly that's so hard. Now go to sleep this minute.'

The morning was a bustle of activity. Mary didn't go to work as usual. Instead she organized us like an efficient little mother. Mam was still in bed. I looked at her flushed face and felt frightened. 'What's wrong, Mam?' I wailed and began to cry. A smile touched her mouth. Her green eyes were very bright. 'Chris, my wee lamb,' she said tenderly, 'don't cry. You've been my baby up till now but there's going to be another. It's going to be born soon. I want you to look after Alec and do as Mary tells you.'

After we had breakfasted on thick porridge and buttery toast we were bundled into the room.

'But have I not to go to school?' cried Kirsty, who was a very well organized little being and liked everything to run in its usual order; also, she took a pride in getting marks for good attendance at school.

'No,' said Mary, 'you're to stay in case you're needed to go for messages. I've got to help Mam so you and Ian will have to look after the wee ones.'

Ian sniggered, positively revelling in the prospect of a day off school. His blue eyes shone in his sunburned face and Alec and I squirmed, not relishing a day under our big brother's regime.

'Behave yerselves or I'll hear aboot it,' warned Da, his voice less menacing without the influence of drink.

'You'd best get to work, Da,' said Mary. 'The midwife will be here soon and you'll only get in the way.'

Normally she would never have dared order him to do anything, but today was an exception.

'There's the door,' said Ian, rushing to admit a small woman dressed in green. She had delivered quite a few of us and had told Mam I ought to be the last. She glowered at Da, who ably returned the look, and she flounced past him into the kitchen.

Mam was beginning to moan quite loudly. We draped ourselves about the room, eyeing each other in unspoken dread.

'Rotten babies!' said Ian, his memory able to take him back to similar times. 'Mam should stop having them. They're noisy and smelly.' He looked at me. '*You* were really smelly. I had to clean your bum sometimes. I thought after you Mam wouldn't have any more.'

Terror at my Mam's plight, combined with rage, made me brave. 'I wasn't smelly!' I cried passionately 'And – and you *never* had to clean my bum. I *never* had to wear nappies. I was never a baby like you. You should *still* be wearing nappies 'cos you mess up your drawers all the time . . .'

'Be quiet,' said Kirsty. 'C'mon, out to play, all of you.'

The backcourts were bereft of the usual bustle because all our friends were at school. Every so often Mary popped her head from the window requesting Ian or Kirsty to run for a message. Lunch consisted of thick slices of bread and jam thrown down from the kitchen window. We set off to the Elder Park, our gloom dispelling at the idea of an afternoon guddling about by the little boating pond. The baby still hadn't arrived by tea-time but the birth wasn't far off. Hungry and resentful of babies in general, we argued among ourselves in the room. Kirsty was allowed the breath-taking honour of going through to the kitchen to heat water, leaving us with Ian who grabbed the opportunity to show us how masterful he was. He made us sit on the floor, cross-legged, arms folded, daring us to move a muscle or speak.

We heard Da clumping in from work and ten muscle-cramped minutes later he put his head round the door. 'Come on ben,' he said, a hint of pride in his steel-blue eyes. 'Yer mother wants ye to see yer new sister.'

'A girl!' snorted Ian.

'Ay,' returned Da. 'Thank God we've no' another yin like you.'

We trooped into the kitchen. It smelt of disinfectant and steam. Mam looked exhausted, with blue shadows under her eyes. The new arrival was snuggled into a shawl at her side. Ian gave it no more than a cursory glance, then turned away. Da lifted Alec up to have a look, then he grabbed me in his strong arms. I stared at the baby's red face. It yawned widely, exposing pink gums.

'Do you like your wee sister?' asked Mam.

'It's got an awful wrinkled face and it's baldy,' I said disgustedly, feeling a pang of jealousy as Mam cuddled the baby to her breast.

'It's likely done it already,' I stated bluntly.

'Done what?' asked Mam.

'Shat itself,' I said, with an evil chuckle which died in my throat at the feel of Da's heavy hand across my upturned bottom. He despised such talk unless he was in the mood for it. If Mam used such words he couldn't help laughing because she made them sound so funny. She was forty years old when she gave birth to Margaret. She had spent a lot of her life bearing and rearing children. At barely eighteen she had given birth to her first son. Another son and two daughters were to follow before she was widowed at just twenty-seven. It wasn't for us to wonder why she had married Da, who was thirty years her senior, a widower with a grown-up family scattered around the globe. In retrospect he must have been a pillar to lean on, someone to man a house full of dependent children.

But he had been the means of swelling the family even further, till now we numbered nine. Seventy when Margaret was born, he had the bearing of a young man. His iron-grey hair was thick, his eyesight so good he disdained the use of glasses except for reading. He had fought through the Boer War and the Great War and was a man's man, tough of body, resilient of spirit, unable to understand anyone whose power of will wasn't as indomitable as his own. He expected his offspring to reflect his strength of character and found it in all but Alec, whose nervous manner and hesitant speech constantly annoyed him.

Fortunately we had also inherited Mam's sensitivity to temper our stubborn natures. None of us was close to Da in those early days. The age gap was too great to be bridged by the usual forms of communication. Because Mam was always so busy we had no one to turn to for advice on school work and personal matters, so we looked to each other and were close-knit brothers and sisters, though we niggled so much at each other.

Da was a frightening figure to us in our infancy. His drinking petrified us. Weekends were the worst of all. He had more money in his pocket then. We waited fearfully for him to come home, knowing his temper would be fiery, his tongue sharper than a razor. If we didn't get the brunt of it, Mam did. It was terrible to see the sadness in her eyes and the flush of anger on her face. Yet despite her vulnerability, she defended herself and protected us with a tenacity perhaps even greater than Da's because hers was born of love, not stubbornness.

But Da's shell of hardness had many soft spots. He spoiled Mam in different ways. Every Sunday he gave her breakfast in bed, his whole attitude softened. It was his way of making up for his previous night's drinking.

Beyond the tenements were houses where flowers smelt sweetly. In summer we went for long walks, taking up the breadth of the pavement. Da never failed to pluck a rose dangling from a wall. 'There ye are, Evelyn,' he would say to Mam, 'a rose for a rose.'

Because of Mam we laughed a lot together. When Jimmy Shand played on our big, accumulator-operated radio, she grabbed Da and they waltzed round the kitchen. Unable to resist, the rest of us joined in, jigging from kitchen to room in a long crocodile, Da chuckling heartily, Mam's eyes wet with tears of merriment.

After Margaret's birth, Mam remained physically exhausted for a long time and we all had to do our share of work. Though I was only four I soon learned to change Margaret's nappies, taking my displeasure out on the baby by slapping a cold flannel against her little pink buttocks. When she cried in protest, I was quick to turn an innocent face to Mam.

'My, but she's a girny bairn that,' Mam said once.

'Not like I was, Mam,' I said self-righteously.

'No, not like you were, Chris,' said Mam with a smile, 'you were much worse.'

Backcourt Capers

By the time I was six I was an established tomboy and much preferred the company of boys. I scorned girls' games and girls' toys. Dolls were for cissies, cars and trains a delight. I was accepted into gangs of boys, included in their wild games. Walls and trees were there to be climbed. I resented the fact that I'd been born a girl and grew furious when the boys teased me because I wore knickers, but could do nothing about it because wearing knickers was infinitely preferable to wearing none.

Our favourite territory was the nearby Elder Park, where we whooped in and out of the bushes brandishing pieces of wood for guns. The park-keeper spent a great deal of his time chasing us and we spent a good deal of ours shouting rude names at him and pulling dreadful faces at a safe distance. One of our most favoured occupations was browsing round the trees looking for caterpillars. If they were scarce in the park we went to nearby gardens to hunt through large nasturtium leaves, sometimes managing to find a nice fat caterpillar before we were chased from the gardens. I loved my caterpillars; not for me silly caterpillar races with the poor little creatures getting poked with sticks if they went in the wrong direction. I preferred to study mine, feeling thrilled at a miracle of nature that had made so many pairs of sticky little legs. The feel of them creeping over my hands was an ecstasy; even when they expelled their minute particles of excreta, I hugged myself with the wonder of it all.

They were housed in a big matchbox which I kept under my pillow. I hoarded them jealously, careful that Da never saw them because he had already broken my heart by throwing some in the fire the previous year. Listening to them popping in the flames I mustered all the powers in me to bring about a similar doom to such a murderer, but my unsavoury wishes never came to fruition.

With the passing of a year I became more cunning where Da was concerned, but I didn't reckon with Kirsty. One day she found me in the room playing with my caterpillars. She was distinctly more lady-like than me and hated creepy-crawlies in any form. She stared at the squirming little creatures, her horror all the keener with the knowledge that she had, in all innocence, been sleeping beside them for nights on end.

'I'm going to tell Da on you,' she said, her disgust making her resort to the most despised threat of all. 'I'll tell if you don't get rid of them. You're a dirty wee bitch!'

'Tell-tale!' I jeered, while racking my brains for another place to keep my pets. Inspiration came with a blinding flash and my eyes sparkled. 'Tell all you like, Lady Kirsty. I don't care. No one's going to find my catties!'

Later that day I crept down to the stairhead lavatory, inserted the key and went inside. It was a square little box of a place, known to our family as 'the cludge'. The walls, cistern and pipes were all painted a dark dingy green. The bare boards of the floor were scrubbed white, with sheets of newspaper spread over them to guard against muddy feet. To the left of the toilet pan was an oblong window with rusty wire mesh over the lower half. One of the panes had been broken by an errant ball and never replaced. A piece of wood was nailed over the space so that there was always half-light in the small enclosure.

This was one of my favourite hideouts, a place of privacy when ever-present humans became too much of a burden. Each tenant on our landing had a key to it; ours hung on a hook just inside the door in the lobby. It was here I came to scrutinize the pages of the *Sunday Post*. Perched comfortably on the wooden toilet seat, I chuckled with glee at the antics of 'The Broons' and 'Oor Wullie'.

When I genuinely wanted to use the toilet I amused myself reading little snippets from the neat squares of paper that were threaded through with string and tied to a nail on the door. These squares were used by our family in the course of our needs, except for Mam who preferred something of a gentler nature and armed herself with fistfuls of tissue paper on her excursions to the cludge.

Our neighbours distinguished themselves by being able to afford real toilet paper and one lady had asked Mam to remove the newspaper squares because they brought down the tone of the toilet. The 'posh' landings above ours took it in turns to hang neat rolls of paper in their toilets and our neighbour was anxious for our landing to follow the same principle. But her pleas were in vain and, little devils that we were, we tore huge bundles of squares, waited till the lady appeared from her lavender-smelling house, then trooped downstairs, gaily trailing streams of paper tied in such a way that they resembled the paper bows in the tail of a kite. We were known as 'the Fraser tribe' in our area and must have been a great nuisance to our neighbours. Our 'Toilet Paper Lady', as we had wickedly christened her, appeared to regard her trips to the lavatory as an altogether shameful business. She glided down on noiseless slippers, tried the door and, if it was locked, crept back upstairs again to await a later chance. I knew she watched through her keyhole for the coast to be clear and delayed my exit from the cludge as long as possible. Always I waited till she was forced to try the door again, then I would shout in a voice full of innocence, 'I'm just coming.' When I finally emerged, it was my joy to summon Alec to the lobby where we took turns peeping through the keyhole to watch the lady's head gradually come round the crack in her door;

then, seeing no one, she would go bolting red-faced downstairs.

We also made full use of 'Chanty Emptying' times. With no lavatory in the house, there was nothing else to do but use a chamber pot during the night. In the morning we made no pretence of hiding it on the way to emptying it down the toilet, but our Toilet Paper Lady had more finesse about the whole business and would only cart her chamber pot to the toilet during quiet spells on the landing. Occasionally we took it into our heads to waylay her and jostled each other at the lobby keyhole till she emerged. At the crucial moment one of us opened our door and looked out, completely unnerving the poor lady so that she almost dropped her discreetly covered chamber.

Kirsty and Ian were too grown up for such pranks and Alec simply followed me in everything so it was I who incurred the most displeasure in the Toilet Paper Lady.

But she was far from my mind that day I sought a new home for my caterpillars. Carefully I deposited the box on top of the cistern. It took a good deal of effort for, although I was tall for my age, it wasn't easy to reach up to the damp, flat surface above the pipes, even though I stood on the toilet seat to gain height. But the act was accomplished and I hugged myself with glee. My catties were safe and my satisfaction was complete. For the next few days I was never away from the cludge and Mam asked anxiously if I had diarrhoea.

The neighbours spoke in muted whispers about 'that wee devil, Chris', surely the wildest member of the Fraser tribe. All went well for almost a week. I made many trips to local gardens for fresh leaves, watching with breathless wonder while my catties nibbled holes, climbed round my fingers, and marched up the cistern pipes for exercise.

Then catastrophe struck. A knock came to our door. The Toilet Paper Lady stood there. 'Mrs Fraser,' she said to Mam, 'do you know anything about these horrible things in the toilet?'

Two-year-old Margaret squirmed in Mam's arms and held out a chubby fist. 'Ball! Gimme ball!' she chuckled and tried to grab our neighbour's severe bun. This didn't help to improve her mood. She glowered at Margaret and stepped back a pace.

'I don't know what you mean, Mrs Murdoch,' said Mam in her delightful Aberdonian accent. Sometimes she deliberately accentuated it so that it was difficult for the untrained ear to fully understand her. The Toilet Paper Lady glared. I hid with Alec behind Mam's back and waited with bated breath.

'I mean these beasties! All over the place. Come down and see for yourself.'

We followed Mam at a safe distance. Alec was in the secret with me and his nervous discomfort was perhaps even greater than mine when we saw a gallant army of striped caterpillars marching out from the gap under the cludge door.

'Oh my,' said Mam calmly, 'caterpillars!'

Our neighbour's lips folded into a tight line. 'Ay, very perceptive of you, Mrs Fraser! Caterpillars! In the toilet! It's a disgrace! I couldn't believe my eyes when one crawled over my knee just as . . .' she floundered and blushed scarlet as if she had been on the verge of giving away a trade secret.

Mam glanced at us; we stared at the shiny brown banister with great interest. There was no doubt she knew we were the culprits. Her family was the youngest on the landing. The Toilet Paper Lady had a grown-up daughter and a teenage son, our other neighbour had one very adult son. No matter how fanciful one's imagination might be, it just wasn't possible to picture any of them hoarding catties in the cludge.

Mam shook her head. 'It's gey funny,' she said, her accent so pronounced that even we could hardly understand. 'But I'll tell you what I'll do, Mrs Murdoch, I'll get my bairns to gather them up for you and take them away.'

'For *me*?' exploded the Toilet Paper Lady.

'Ay,' returned Mam pleasantly. 'You wouldny like them left in there, would you now?'

Well! Wasn't our Mam devious? Mrs Murdoch emitted a gigantic snort before stomping upstairs and into her house without another word. Mam gave me a slow and deliberate wink. Wasn't that mother love for you?

'Right, you two,' she twinkled, 'gather up your

caterpillars and put them among the flowers where they belong. Don't be long, your tea's nearly ready.'

The thought of Da's fat, golden chips comforted me slightly. Sadly I picked up my beloved catties and with Alec trailing at my heels took them to a nearby garden. Soon they were lost in a forest of nasturtium leaves. A face peeked suspiciously from a window. Despite my sorrow I couldn't help sniggering wickedly at the idea of my catties rampaging through the garden, devouring all the Tom Thumbs in sight.

We wandered home.

'I wonder how they got out from the box,' said Alec.

'It was an old matchbox,' I said regretfully. 'Maybe the vibration of the chain made it open and they all went marching down the pipes.' I giggled, 'Can you imagine old Toilet Paper's face when one clumped over her knee? I bet she couldn't get her knickers up fast enough.'

'Wash yer hands!' commanded Da the minute we were inside. He was retired now and a good help about the house. Mary had recently married, and Ian was away at a home in the country because of his weak chest, so our house was not as crowded as in recent years. We were still a family of six, however, a handful in the cramped quarters of room and kitchen, so Da's help was more than needed in our busy home.

After a line-up for hand inspection we all gathered round the table. Only Mam and Da had chairs; the rest of us had to stand. We were not allowed to speak during mealtimes, but we got up to all the usual childish tricks; eyeing each other; kicking under the table; stifling back fits of laughter. The agony of choking back merriment under Da's stern eye lives with me still.

It was a lengthy meal when Da's crispy chips were included in the menu. Second helpings were a must, lavishly sprinkled with salt and vinegar. Scottish dance music flowed from the wireless. At the end of the meal Mam seized a spoon and began tapping it against the surrounding crockery. Each cup, each plate, produced a different note full of a primitive rhythm.

Before long we were all tapping away merrily. The kitchen was gay with tinkling sounds. Da watched with an expressionless face, shaking his head occasionally to signify that we were all quite mad.

After a few minutes Mam brought us down to earth. 'Right, Chris,' she said firmly, 'it's your turn to do the dishes.'

'But I did them this morning,' I muttered, unwilling to tackle the distasteful chore without a fight.

'I did them this morning!' cried Kirsty.

'You never did! You only cleared the table!'

We went at each other till Da quelled us with a mighty roar. 'Right! That's enough! Chris, you get in there! Do as yer mother tells ye and no' another word!'

I skulked into the scullery. 'It's not fair,' I whispered under my breath so that I could have the satisfaction of the last word.

'Can I go out to play?' I asked, when the last cup had been hung on its hook.

‘Ay, but don’t be late in,’ said Mam.

Alec clattered downstairs at my side. The old air-raid shelters in the backcourts were the rendezvous for gang gatherings. Here, in the damp, musty caverns, concoctions of mischief had their beginnings, magical plans took shape.

It was a hot night in July, and outdoor games were decided upon. After we had exhausted the list the old favourite of hide-and-seek took us in and out of closes, abandoned wash-houses, all kinds of nooks and crannies. Dusk approached. We all waited with a tingling apprehension for a warning cry to echo down the backcourts.

‘Sandshoe Harry! Sandshoe Harry!’

No one had ever seen Sandshoe Harry. He was a phantom who walked hand in hand with night. Whenever his name was mentioned the thrill of fear tingled the spine, childish imaginings were stretched to the limit. After the hour of dusk no one dared go near the air-raid shelters. Ghostly apparitions lurked in yawning black spaces, ready to pounce on the unwary wanderer.

Now we lolled in home-made hammocks strung between corner railings. They were a concoction of rope and tatty coats, arranged in such a way that the weight of our bodies kept them intact. Oh, the glory of lying there! Swinging lazily back and forth. After a long wait in the queue it was my turn for a hammock. The evening breeze fanned my hot dusty cheeks and I looked up at the misty blue sky. Something in my child's mind stirred to an awareness of the beauty in that patch of blue. Grey towers of chimneys were silhouetted against puff-ball clouds. It wasn't difficult for me to imagine that the grey chimneys were spires of fairy castles piercing into the cotton-wool clouds. I drifted and dreamed, no longer inhaling the odour of stale cooking from the surrounding houses. Instead I remembered the sweet scent of new-cut grass in the park and sniffed in the imagined smell of it, letting it mingle with my fairy castles and my blue sky.

'It's my turn,' whined Alec at my elbow.

'Och . . . you!' I scolded, letting him into the hammock only to swing him violently. He yelled so loudly I was afraid he would bring Da to the window.

Darkness descended gently and our dread of Campbell's Close made us desert the backcourts for the comparative brightness of the front street. It was a corner close, a shortcut through to another street, but we only dared use it in the daytime. It was full of twists and little dark corners that neither daylight nor flickering gaslight ever reached. The spiral stairs seemed to reach upwards and onwards into outer space, making it a challenge to the spirit to ascend up to the first flight.

The name of the close so intrigued me that I made up stories of murders and other gory deeds which I attributed to the legendary Campbell, my ability to scare the wits out of my pals satiating me with power. But I was only brave enough to recount such tales in the benign light of day.

The streets were quietening now; shadows leapt in the closes. In a tight knot we gathered at the close mouth to plead with Mick Mulligan to tell us a story. Mick was older than the rest of us, perhaps fourteen or fifteen, but his magnetic gift for spinning fantasies bridged the gap of years. He was tall and very thin with blue eyes shining vividly in a tanned, grimy face. He lived in one of the little houses that had a door in from the street and the filth and poverty of his home was the talk of the district. Mam had warned us not to go too near Mick in case we got fleas. Mice sometimes leapt out of the window. One had actually bitten me when I was jumping on the low stone walls surrounding the house.

'Even the mice canny bear the guff in that house,' Mam had said.

Mick lived with his parents and his grandfather in the tiny single apartment. Beds were made up from old chairs, newspapers and tattered coats served as blankets. If our gang was at a loose end we passed the time by jumping up and down on the wall to try and get a glimpse in through the grimy window. Once I saw old Grandfather lying on two chairs covered with a coat. The street held its breath whenever the Sanitary Inspector tried to gain entry inside. He would have rapped his knuckles raw and never got an answer. The occupants used special knocks to signify who they were. The sounds that came from the house on Saturday nights were alarming. Unintelligible shouts and screams floated into the street. Grandfather was nearly always drunk, yet he was the kindliest old man imaginable, ever ready with a nice word for children. We all liked him, yet dreaded his passing us in the close with his 'jobby bucket', an enamel pail filled to the brim with nauseous contents. On his way to empty it in the lavatory at the close back he would put out a filthy paw and pat each of us gently on the head. Kirsty always cringed away from him, her face crimson with revulsion at the idea of his hands near her beautiful shining hair. The rest of us smiled sweetly but the minute he was out of sight we waited with bated breath for the great sludging sound of his bucket being emptied down the cludge, then we would erupt into helpless giggles.

Mick was cleaner than Grandfather, but it wasn't unusual to see parts of his anatomy peeping from the back of his pants. We cared not about his appearance. His sense of fun, his sensitive nature, carried him far above his impoverished existence and he was beloved by every child in the neighbourhood. He took us into other realms with his tales. I was a bedtime storyteller, holding sway over Kirsty and Alec, but Mick, because of his age and self-confidence, was able to command a bigger audience.

'Don't shout now, Da,' I said to myself in the midst of a fabled land of wonder.

'Da's at the window,' Alec reported nervously.

'Keep in,' I ordered, but it was too late. Da's usual bellow soared from above.

'We're coming,' I shouted half-heartedly. Before venturing upstairs, I quickly examined my shoes, which were in a dreadful state after slopping through muddy puddles, climbing dykes and kicking stones. 'I'll have to give them a wipe,' I told Alec. 'You'd better do yours as well.'

We repaired to a nearby puddle and dipped in screwed-up balls of newspaper which we applied to our shoes. Then we dashed upstairs before the temporary water-shine wore away, praying they would escape attention till the nightly polish and spit faked up all the scuffs. We marched into the kitchen. We always marched because if you slunk Da immediately suspected something was amiss.

The shoe last was out. Da was obviously embarked on a shoe-repairing session. I shook in my squelching shoes. Horror piled on horror when I looked down and saw my rapidly drying shoes turning a dull streaky grey before my eyes.

'Right, you two,' he said, not looking up from the last, his specs hanging on the tip of his nose. 'Get yer shoes off till I see if they're needin' a seg or two.'

Alec looked at me in panic. Kirsty, sitting with her bare feet, looked at us smugly, knowing that her shoes, like the rest of her attire, were immaculate.

Mam, sitting quietly in her hard little chair crocheting

a beautiful rainbow bedspread, saw our dilemma and put her work to one side.

'Come into the scullery, you two,' she said softly. 'The dishes weren't washed properly at teatime so you'll do the cups all over again.'

'That's right, Evelyn,' applauded Da, hammering with gusto. 'You tell them!'

Once in the scullery Mam turned on the tap and whispered, 'Quick, get your shoes off and give them a lick of polish. They're a disgrace, but I don't want any bawling matches tonight.' Raising her voice for Da's benefit she said, 'Come on, get that cup washed, Chris. Next time you might no' be in such a hurry.'

She swished water round in the sink while we got out the polish. The shoes were duly presented to Da who gave them an incredulous examination. Fortunately for us he had no sense of smell so couldn't detect the strong fumes of polish. 'They're helluva clean lookin',' he said. 'They look like they've jist been polished.'

'Och, Da,' I smirked innocently. 'It's just that we weren't playing much tonight. Mick was telling us stories.'

'Ye'll get fleas aff that fella,' said Da and I knew I'd said the wrong thing. 'I told ye tae stay away from him. Don't tell me you spent a whole night listening tae a lot o' rubbish. Are ye sickening for something? Maybe like lazyitis!'

We stood at the table sipping our cocoa, letting him go rambling on between a mouthful of nails.

'Mick's a fine loon,' said Mam gently. 'He should have been born into the gentry, so he should. He has a refined face . . . no' like his parents at all.'

'Ay, well, he's maybe had a different faither for all we know,' said Da significantly. 'But it doesny change the fact he reeks like a sewer.'

'Well, goodnight, Mam, goodnight, Da,' I said hastily, escaping through to the room before Da decided that we weren't to hob-nob with Mick again.

'We're all to go to the shows tomorrow,' volunteered Kirsty when we were lying in bed. There was plenty of space in the big brass bed now that Ian was away. Margaret slept on a chair-bed in the kitchen and Alec had the recess vacated by Mary. 'Don't tell Mam I told you,' continued Kirsty. 'Because she wasn't going to say anything to you till tomorrow. She gets sick of you two pestering her with questions long before we ever get to a place.'

In my excitement at hearing the news I ignored the somewhat superior tone of her voice. 'The shows,' I breathed reverently while Alec's words came falling over each other from the recess. 'When did Mam tell you? Are we all going? Is Da going?'

'We're all to go,' said Kirsty calmly. 'Even Margaret, though she's too wee to know much. It was Da suggested it for an anniversary treat for Mam. It means he won't be able to go drinking tomorrow night because he won't have much money left after the shows.'

We spent the next half hour discussing all the wonderful attractions that the annual fair, held at Glasgow Green, had to offer. Every so often we paused to shout, 'Goodnight, Mam,' waiting with love in our hearts for the beloved voice to filter reassuringly through the wall. It took a great deal of restraint for us not to ask any questions next day. The morning passed slowly but eventually we were all on the tram, excitement oozing from us with every turn of the wheels.

The hot, dusty fairground was a place of magic, a wonderland of bustling happiness. My eyes tried to take it all in at once, Alec's breath came out in tight little puffs, Kirsty looked with serene yearning at the cheap jewellery displayed in colourful profusion everywhere. But none of us asked our parents for anything that wasn't offered. It was treat enough to be there, to feel part of the fun-filled world. Music blared, people screamed from huge mechanical monsters that zoomed around in dizzy whirls of motion. There was a maze of side-shows, and we were given three pennies each to spend as we wished.

Da hoisted a pop-gun to his shoulder and took aim at a row of clay faces on a conveyor-belt. He was a striking figure in his best suit, his watch-chain sparkling against a maroon silk waistcoat. I thought he looked at ease with the gun held so expertly, but at six years old I was too young to realize he must have been familiar with real guns in his younger days. To me, war was just stories that Da told us when he was in the mood, amusing stories to suit a young audience; never once did he touch on the real horror of things he must have experienced. He pulled at the trigger and I held my breath. Pop! Pop! Pop! went the gun.

'Da's won something!' I shouted, staring in joyful disbelief when he was handed a scraggy monkey on a string.

He handed it to Mam, his face transformed in a smile of benevolence. 'There ye are, Evelyn, a wee mascot for the mantelpiece.'

Margaret stretched out a chubby fist to grab the dangling monkey and the rest of us looked on enviously when she was allowed to hold it.

Alec and I wandered along together. Everything was full of delight on such a day. Da's mood was such that we dared to pass several comments that would normally have been received with sour acclaim.

Pink candy floss was much in evidence and our mouths watered profusely.

'It looks like rotten cotton wool,' I growled and Alec nodded feebly.

'Away and get some o' that pink stuff,' said Da unexpectedly.

'For everyone?' gasped Kirsty, and Da nodded jovially.

I buried my face into the flimsy textured candy, feeling my happiness was complete, till Da reached out a horny hand and took my free hand in his. Well! I had never known such a thing to happen before! I held his dry, hard hand, hardly allowing myself to breathe for fear of a reprimand.

When every possible corner of the fairground had been explored, we walked to the edge of the Green where barrows were piled high with mouth-watering fruit.

'Get the bairns a bag of plums, John,' said Mam persuasively. He grumbled for a few moments, then dug into his pocket to count his money. 'I'll get them, Da,' I piped, anxious in case he decided his pocket wouldn't stretch to a further luxury. He dropped some silver into my outstretched palm and I sped to the barrows. Two paper bags were filled to the brim with juicy Victoria plums. With guilt tearing me in two I popped one in my mouth, gulping it down so quickly I almost choked on the stone, then I hastened red-faced to where my family stood in a tight little knot.

'Right now, Kirsty,' said Da, 'you sit on this bench and share oot the plums. I'm taking yer mother for a glass of port. We'll no' be long. See and watch Maggie.'

'Right, Da.' Kirsty was already intent on counting out the plums, the rest of us hovering beside her to make sure she counted right. Alec's eyes glimmered with tears because he thought Kirsty had given herself more than anyone else. Patiently she counted them all over again. We sat with the heaps of plums in our laps, childishly unwilling to begin eating them because then the treat would be over.

We sat in the sun, slowly eating our plums, our beings satiated with the rare pleasures of such a day.

'Da was good this afternoon,' I said wonderingly.

Kirsty nodded. 'Ay, and he won't have the money to go drinking tonight so there won't be any trouble.'

Mam and Da were coming back. Mam's green eyes were sparkling and she was holding on to Da's arm. They looked intimate and happy. Somewhere at the back of my young mind I realized they had a contentment with each other despite their ups and downs.

We couldn't bear Da when he was drunk and made Mam cry, but there were times it was easy to see that, in his own strange way, he adored her as much as we did.

Chatterina Tottie Scone

In winter the grey tenements piled up into grey skies. Blurring rain and early darkness forced us to seek indoor pursuits. Yet winter was my favourite time when I was a child. There was a cosiness about it, a feeling of unity in the family circle. There were also so many winter events that it was altogether a very exciting time.

First of all there was Hallowe'en. Weeks before the witching night we discussed, argued, and fought over our respective ideas for dressing up. When the big night came we were off, long dresses tripping us, faces bright with rouge and lipstick, armed with lap-bags made by Kirsty at school which we hoped to fill with spoils.

Sometimes we took short cuts to different streets via the backcourts, quiet, dark stretches full of shadows. It was easy for me to conjure up visions of witches flying over the sky on broomsticks. Wickedly I exaggerated my flights of fancy out of all proportion till Alec was reduced to a gibbering mess and Kirsty told me she would never go anywhere with me again.

When we returned home we were eager to share the 'takings' with our parents. Da was very fond of apples and at Hallowe'en we were able to give him some big rosy ones which he sniffed appreciatively before putting them away in his drawer. This was where he kept all his little bits and pieces. It was kept locked so that our prying fingers wouldn't discover his secrets. When he unlocked it glorious smells tumbled out – tobacco, apples, leather, all mingled together to produce an oddly pleasing fragrance.

As soon as Hallowe'en was over we began to prepare eagerly for Christmas. The table was pulled out from the wall and we gathered round to make paper-chains and sparkling balls from silver paper. In those early days we couldn't afford the luxury of a tree, but the house was made jolly with our home-made decorations.

We were very responsible travellers for young children and now that I was eight I was allowed to go into town with Alec for Christmas shopping. We were both experts at dodging our fare on the tram. During the journey we were angelically quiet and sat with our noses pressed against the window. Cunningly we always chose a nice comfortable housewife to sit beside so that her many shopping bags and voluminous clothes would swallow us into anonymity. Frequently the ruse was successful. When it came to our stop we quickly hopped from the vehicle, unable to resist shouting after it, 'Ha! Ha! We never paid our fa-are!'

Armed with shopping lists we mingled with the crowds in the big stores, our course of action well planned. Removing my large pixie hood from my head I dropped it over some small article which I picked up inside the hood. To put it bluntly, I was a little thief. Alec sniffed nervously at my side, but I marched along with confidence, bullying him into being my accomplice, daring him to say anything that might fall on the ears of authority.

I had few feelings of guilt. The things I took were for a family I loved. There were so few luxuries in our lives yet there seemed to be so many everywhere else. My philosophy, as an eight-year-old, rather poor child, was that Christmas was a time for giving and, no matter how, I was going to give to my beloved Mam the things she deserved to enrich her humdrum existence.

I can remember the Christmas of 1951 very vividly. On Christmas Eve our excitement was tremendous. We plagued Da for a loan of his longest socks even though we knew we would be lucky if they were only partially filled. The stockings were hung carefully at the end of each bed and we lay in the dark room talking about the magic of Christmas. Later, when our ponderings and anticipations were exhausted, my mind was in a suitably productive state to recount a magical tale to Alec and Margaret.

Kirsty no longer slept in the room with us. She shared the double bed in the kitchen with Mam, and Da slept in our old brass bed just inside the kitchen door. This arrangement had no doubt been made by Mam for fear of adding another to the family, but thoughts like that didn't enter our heads. It was just another arrangement and, as far as I was concerned, a very satisfactory one. I now slept quite alone in a single iron bed, a hand-down from a neighbour. It was an old bed but very comfortable and I felt so important I might have looked down my nose at royalty if it had chanced along.

Margaret's chair-bed was alongside mine and Alec still slept in the recess.

Most nights I spun yarns for their benefit, always beginning, 'Once upon a time there lived a family called Fraser. They were of noble blood and lived in a castle with spires that reached up into the sky, so high that they tore the clouds to pieces and made the rain come.'

At this point I knew to expect the usual cries of protest from my audience.

'We don't live in a castle,' said Alec unfailingly. 'We live in a tenement with a cludge on the landing and sometimes fleas on us from Mick Mulligan!'

'That's right,' Margaret added eagerly. 'We don't have fairy spears.'

'Spires,' I corrected scornfully, knowing that their objections were merely a dare to my abilities as a storyteller. It was up to me to take them out of reality into realms of fantasy and my stories so convinced them that Margaret would cry with the beauty of her imagined life in a fairy castle and Alec would sniff for a few moments then plead eagerly for more. At Christmas my tales had to be extra special and I spun yarns about snow and magic stars till I fell asleep with sheer exhaustion.

We were too wise in the ways of the world to believe the fable about Santa Claus. Nevertheless we pretended to each other there was 'something in it all' and on the Eve of Christmas tried to stay awake long enough just to find out what that something was, but we never could keep our eyes open long enough to see the shadowy figure of Mam creeping about filling our stockings.

On Christmas morning we grabbed the bumpy exciting stockings, thrilled to find tangerines, apples and perhaps a pencil case or a book. Right at the toe there was usually a silver sixpence or a pencil sharpener.

Still in vests and knickers we trooped through the lobby with our eyes shining, hoping to witness the grand opening of our parents' parcels. We always insisted they hung stockings too and really Da must have been quite a sport to allow a long woolly sock to dangle from his bedhead.

That morning of Christmas '51 Da was sitting up in bed, dressed in his 'simmit' and a pair of long drawers, smoking his pipe, and looking not the least interested in finding out the contents of his stocking.

We had scrimped for weeks to get him an ounce of his favourite tobacco and a large box of matches, and our annoyance at his lack of curiosity was intense.

Mam was entirely different. She poked and delved

with great enthusiasm and we watched with bated breath while she pulled out a cheap bottle of perfume and a new apron.

'From Alec and Chris,' she said quietly and I saw that her eyes were very bright, the way they went when she was about to cry.

'I got you something too, Mam,' said Kirsty, handing over a brightly wrapped package. She looked at me suspiciously, obviously wondering how I'd managed to get Mam the gifts. She wasn't in the secret of the 'magic pixie', the fable I'd invented to salve my conscience. I'd likened my red pixie to the hen that kept on laying golden eggs, only my pixie needed a little help from me to get it working.

The week after Christmas was busy and jolly. New Year was Da's favourite time and he liked the house to be clean. We scrubbed shelves and polished dusty corners, Da cleaned all the windows and got out big tins of distemper to brighten the walls. Mam washed the floors under the bed recesses then Da painted them with paraffin. This was done to keep away bed bugs, horrible little insects with the feeding habits of vampires. We were seldom bothered with them because of Da's diligent applications of paraffin. The house reeked with the strong fumes but it was far better to suffer that than the other menace.

The day before Hogmanay Kirsty got out the black lead and polished the range till it gleamed like black satin.

The house was full of the smells of baking. Every day some new fragrance titillated the senses. Trays of shortbread, black bun and fruit cake were set on the table to cool. Oh to savour just a scrap, but it was all to be kept for the big night.

On Hogmanay all the glasses were brought down from the shelves to be washed and polished till they sparkled. The table was set with mouth-watering goodies and a bottle of whisky gleamed amber in the firelight. Da had bought it with money sent from a son of his former marriage who lived in the awesomely far land of Australia. He was older than Mam. We had met him several times when he came back to Scotland for a holiday and we simply called him 'Uncle Jack', the thought never entering our heads that a man older than Mam was actually our half brother.

The evening was gay and festive. The kitchen resounded with Scottish dance music and we whirled about to the merry tunes.

Much to our chagrin we had to go to bed as usual, but we made it a policy that year to stay awake till the bells heralded in the New Year. Sleep threatened but excitement kept it at bay. Tunes from the wireless floated through the walls, then the chimes of Big Ben struck out the hour. I couldn't understand the strange choked-up feeling that welled into my throat. Another year, a new year, lay ahead. The room door was thrown open and Mam came in, sparkling-eyed, her auburn hair falling in waves around her face. Behind her came

Da, jovial and kind, all the sternness gone from him as the first glass of whisky warmed his blood. But we knew he wouldn't get drunk. He never did at New Year, which was odd; it seemed such a perfect opportunity for him to indulge. It may have been that the first-foots would be arriving soon. He kept his good side for friends and relations. As man of the house, he perhaps felt it his duty to set a good example.

We wished each other a happy New Year. Mam kissed us, Da shook our hands brusquely. Kirsty came through and sat on the end of my bed while Da poured fruit wine and Mam handed round slabs of black bun and fingers of shortbread.

Solemnly we clinked glasses together, but before we could take a sip of the ruby wine in our glasses we waited patiently for Da to raise his glass in a toast, one he gave us every year. Raising his glass to the ceiling he intoned, 'May ye have roast beef when ye're hungry, whisky when ye're dry, pennies when ye're hard up, and heaven when ye die.'

'That's good, Da,' we murmured in dutiful appreciation, then sipped quickly at our wine before he could think of another toast.

Left in the dark room once more we wished each other the season's greetings over and over till Da bawled at us from the kitchen. We fell asleep in crumpled heaps, but all night we were aware of people clumping in the lobby and laughing in the kitchen.

In January the snow came, turning the dingy tenements into the beautiful fairy palaces of my imagination. Huge snowmen dominated the backcourts, decorated with old bonnets and long scarves, precious bits of coal and clay pipes.

The snow didn't stay clean for long in the well-trodden play areas, but we hurled grey snowballs, made grey snowmen and slithered about joyfully till the rain came and washed the snow away.

Indoor pastimes were many and varied. Sprawled on the room floor we made intricate jigsaws which kept us amused for hours. When we tired of this we went into the kitchen to settle round the table to draw. Mam invariably offered a threepenny bit for a prize and the clock ticked quietly as we concentrated on winning.

When Ian was home the rest of us didn't stand a chance. He was a meticulous artist, giving his drawings a look of realism that none of us could match.

But I had perfected the character of Mighty Mouse till my drawings were in great demand at school. The hours spent in the classroom were a great trial for me. I enjoyed English, art, and spelling – I was frequently the winner of a small prize in spelling competitions – but all other subjects came up against a mental block. I particularly dreaded mental arithmetic when the class was taken by Miss Black, the headmistress. She was an ogre in the disguise of a homo sapiens. She was small in stature, with greying hair cut in a mannish style and odd, amber eyes that sent red-hot sparks into space.

I was always incurring her displeasure because of my untidy appearance and once I had nearly died of humiliation when she came marching into my class with Kirsty attached to her arm. Miss Black placed Kirsty squarely in front of the class and asked us to look at a perfect example of neatness. Kirsty was lovely, from her neatly plaited hair to her polished shoes. Squirming several inches down in my seat I endeavoured to polish my scuffed shoes on my socks and nearly broke my legs in the process. Miss Black's eyes sought me out and a shower of sparks descended on me.

'Kirsty Fraser,' said Miss Black tightly, 'is an example of the neatness I would like to see in *all* my children! There is utterly no need for untidy hair . . .' Here she glared at my locks escaping the ribbons Mam had tied in them that morning. 'No need for sloppy clothes, no matter how old they may be they ought to be worn with dignity.' Here I writhed inside a jersey I had torn at playtime. 'And only a tramp has an excuse for dusty shoes.' At this point I tried to make my shoes disappear by sticking my legs under the seat of the desk in front.

'Come along, Kirsty,' said Miss Black hustling my red-faced sister from the room. An audible sigh of relief escaped the class. Miss Black was widely respected throughout the school, her method of administering the tawse being feared by even the toughest of pupils. She always handed out a 'Doubler', which meant getting the belt with the hands crossed. If reflex action made you draw your hands away she made you rest them on a desk so that she could get a direct hit. So heartily did she swing the deadly weapon that her little skirt billowed outwards at the back and the fortunates who weren't receiving punishment very subtly tried to get a glimpse of her long-legged knickers. It was a slight satisfaction to know that while you squirmed under the stinging blows of the tawse, she was exposing her baggy drawers with every move of her muscular arms.

When she fired mental arithmetic questions like bullets from a gun I came out in a cold sweat. Up, down, up, down, we went, fumbling over a question which, if not answered immediately, was passed on to the next pupil. Always I prayed that my neighbour would be unable to answer a question because it gave me a chance to get my curdled grey matter into focus. Oh, the joy of giving a correct answer! The incredible feeling of disbelief at earning some praise from that awesome little woman! She was the witch in my bed-time stories, only I added four feet to her height and endowed her with several warts. But being a cunning little beggar I made sure Miss Black never found out about my drawings of Mighty Mouse. All the boys wanted one and I perfected them under cover of school books, charging the magnificent sum of a half-penny for each one.

I was constantly racking my brains for ways to make

money, and it was at this time I decided to try my hand at making counterfeit money. Our district abounded with poky little shops, the kind of places that sold everything. If I had been led into one blindfolded I could have identified it because each one had a distinctive smell. One in particular had a delightful odour of apples, bacon and biscuits. All the smells were fusty, but that only added to the attraction. It was to this shop we were sent for Da's tobacco. The owner was a Miss Carmichael, more ancient than an Egyptian mummy with her rounded shoulders, salt and pepper hair frisking out from a scuffed felt hat held in place with a fearsome pin, and yellow skin liberally sprinkled with warts of different size. One of these was extremely large and balanced so precariously on the tip of her nose that we lived in the hope one day it would fall off and go tumbling amongst the newspapers on the counter. The hat pin was also held in awe; we all felt convinced she was capable of using it to stab cheeky children. The tinkling of her bell brought her shuffling from her back shop to peer suspiciously from short-sighted eyes. The big black cat who sat like a statue on the counter also wore this wary look, an unblinking stare with narrowed pupils squinting in moon-like green orbs.

Da's brand of tobacco was kept in a round tin; a little axe-like machine cut a length from a fragrant black coil. It was a fascinating shop altogether and I enjoyed going there for messages, though Mam wasn't too keen to purchase the fusty-smelling goods. Miss Carmichael seemed a perfect recipient for my counterfeit money. Her eyesight was poor, she peered at everything, the spectacles on the end of her nose seemed to afford little aid. It wasn't unusual for her to ask the value of the coins we pushed over the counter. There was no doubt that she was the perfect victim for my hard-hearted little scheme.

I spent an intensely laborious evening covering a penny with silver paper, making the marking come through by rubbing carefully with a thumb nail. The finished product looked very like a half-crown and I crowed with satisfaction.

Next day, Da told me to go to the shop. 'An ounce o' thick black,' he ordered. 'Make sure it's off the roll. I've only a poun' so make sure that blin' wee bat gies ye the right change.'

'Ay, Da,' I said meekly and raced to the shop with Alec at my heels.

'An ounce of thick black,' I said respectfully. Snap! The little axe cut a neat portion and tobacco and change were pushed towards me. Deftly I collected the change, then with a quick sleight-of-hand I placed my 'half-crown' on the counter, requesting sweets which I knew would come to two and sixpence exactly.

Breathlessly we watched the whole transaction. The sweets were placed before us and the penny picked up, receiving no more than a cursory glance before it was put in the drawer.

I gathered up the sweets, keeping an anxious eye on the cat which I fancied was glaring with more malevolence than usual. Out from the shop we flew into a nearby close to stare at each other with mingled triumph and shame.

'What if the polis come after us?' whispered Alec nervously.

'Och, don't be daft,' I said scornfully, angry at him for daring to voice what was already in my own mind. 'How could they trace the penny to us?'

'To you!' said Alec quickly.

'Right! I'll eat all the sweeties if that's how you feel,' I growled, but after a few moments of argument we shared the spoils between us then ran home. Mam was in the scullery and I gave her a bar of chocolate, telling her I had found a shilling. She looked at me suspiciously and I began to have terrible misgivings about the whole affair. What if the police really did come to our door? The awful shame it would bring to my innocent mother was beyond thinking about. I was unable to enjoy my share of the sweets. Any moment I expected a knock at the door heralding the arrival of a big burly policeman complete with notebook. I would be interrogated, asked to account for my doings that day.

I began to make up all sorts of alibis and recounted them to Alec so that his lies would coincide with mine. It was no use! I spent a dreadful day but night came, no policeman appeared, and I began to feel better. I racked my brains for ways to atone for my sins and finally decided to go to Miss Carmichael and offer to do odd jobs for her. Next day I duly presented myself and put my request to her but she looked at me in astonishment and shook her head. 'Na, na, if it's money ye're efter ye'd best go somewhere else.'

'No, I don't want money,' I said earnestly. 'I'm – er . . . working for one of my Brownie badges and must do a week of good deeds.' The glib lie invoked a few moments' stunned silence but I smiled angelically and eventually the old lady said I could sweep the floor. I went to work with a will, brushing great clouds of dust into the air. Miss Carmichael coughed and the cat sneezed so much he fell off the counter to stalk through to the back shop, his tail high in the air. For a whole week I tidied shelves, dusted, and generally cleaned up.

When the week was over I was rather proud of the way I had neatened up the appearance of the shop.

'My, ye've done right well,' approved Miss Carmichael. 'Whit a good wee lassie ye are . . . but then – I always knew Mrs Fraser had nice bairns.'

She handed me two bars of chocolate and a silver sixpence, but I put everything back on the counter and ran from the shop, my conscience clearer than crystal. My career as a coiner had died a very quick death. It was far safer to spend jolly evenings with the gang tying door knobs together in the closes.

When Mick came with us the fun was even more

intense because his ideas were more sophisticated than ours. He stuck bits of chewing gum on to window panes with a thread attached. Buttons went slithering along the thread to rattle at the windows. One awful night a large man ran after us and caught me, shaking me till my teeth rattled. 'Only a *girl* would get caught!' taunted the boys, so to show I was as good as them I joined their cinnamon-smoking parties, puffing with great bravado while I turned green in the dark.

On miserable wet nights we gathered round the range and Mam told us stories about her own childhood. Mostly her tales were of a happy nature, but sometimes her eyes grew sad when she spoke of the lovely countryside of her birthplace. So vivid were her descriptions I could almost see the blue Grampian mountains and hear the rushing waters of the river Dee.

Occasionally we managed to coax her to play for us on the fiddle. Mam had been the youngest of her family and had received certain privileges that her sisters didn't get. One of them had been music lessons on the violin and if she was in the mood she got out the beautiful instrument from its red velvet case. All her favourite tunes filled the kitchen, but the one I liked best was 'Thora'.

'I stand in a land of roses but I dream of a land of snow,' sang Mam and my eyes filled with tears. Her land of roses was very far in the distant past. Years of scrimping had woven silver threads into her lovely burnished hair, yet her eyes remained bright with the love of life. It hadn't yielded much to her in the way of financial perks, but hers was a happiness that went far above materialism. She found pleasure in the simplest things, showing her feelings with a childlike candour that made her seem like a Peter Pan, someone who would never really grow old.

Her attitude rubbed off on all those around her, even on our surly, undemonstrative father who was softening with the passing years. When Mam tired of playing the violin, that was the time for Da to tell his well-worn stories of the war.

'C'mon, Da,' we coaxed till he felt himself to be in such demand our pleas were a challenge to his ego. 'Tell us the one about Chatterina.'

'Right,' he smirked. 'Well, you know that Chatterina was the best mate I had? We went all through the Great War together, never one without the other. One night we were lying aboot in the trenches havin' a wee rest . . . jist talkin' and passing the time like.'

'Ay, Da,' we encouraged.

'Well, we were a lot of poor souls. We were tired that night . . . jist no' as careful as usual. Suddenly a bomb came whizzing down, jist where Chatterina Tottie Scone was sittin'. Can ye guess whit happened then?'

'No, Da!' we chorused, knowing full well what was coming.

'Well, that damt bomb blew Chatterina's heid clean

aff his body. There was Chatterina, no body on his heid, no heid on his body. It was terrible, there his heid lay, jist lookin' at me. Well, out o' the blue one o' the eyes winked at me and I says, "I see ye havny lost yer sense o' humour, Chatterina." There's no' many poor blokes would wink at ye from a blown aff heid . . . is there?'

'No, Da!' we yelled breathlessly, joyfully imagining the gory scene.

'I couldny leave my best mate jist lyin' there,' continued Da. 'So I looked aboot for something that would stick him back together.'

'Just like Humpty Dumpty,' we cried eagerly.

'Ay, but that daft egg never did get mended. The sojers in that story were a wee bit stupid . . . but not me . . . I used my heid and hunted aboot till I found a big pancake a coo had dropped earlier. It was still fine and soft so I scooped it up and used it to stick Chatterina's heid back on his body. He was right as rain after that, never looked back!'

We howled with glee and asked the usual question, 'Did that really happen, Da?'

'Of course, do ye think I'm tellin' lies or something?'

Kirsty smiled with quiet scepticism each time the story was told but the rest of us were never quite sure if such happenings were possible, I in particular dwelling on the scientific aspect of Chatterina's quick repair job, my mind needling into each macabre detail.

I had a very quick and enquiring brain and was always thinking out novel ways to pass dreary winter days. One afternoon we were ensconced in the room, watching dismal rivers of rain running down the window.

'I've got a great idea!' I shouted suddenly, clapping my hands in excitement. Alec and Margaret looked at me with interest but Kirsty was more wary of my madcap schemes.

'Listen to this,' I instructed, rocking myself in a monstrosity of a rocking chair which had been given to us by a friend of Mam's living some distance away. Alec and I had gone to collect it, pushing it all the way home on squeaky castors, stopping every now and then to rock ourselves in the middle of pavements, heedless of the stares of passers-by. 'Let's make up dummy parcels,' I continued, pulling the ends of my long plaits restlessly. 'We can put them on the pavement and watch from the window! It'll be a scream!'

'Och, you're daft!' said Kirsty, but there was a sparkle in her green eyes.

Diving out of the chair I went to the big cupboard to look for a box. 'Get some brown paper and bits of string,' I ordered Alec and he ran through to the kitchen, returning in a few moments with the required items.

'I told Da we were playing pass the parcel,' he said hesitantly.

'Good for you,' I approved while I put all sorts of

rubbish into the box together with a note that read, 'Ha! Ha! Ever been had?'

Kirsty wrapped the box in her meticulous fashion and neatly wrote a fictitious but highly plausible address on the finished parcel. I ran downstairs, took a quick look round to make sure I was unobserved, placed the parcel invitingly on the pavement, then raced back up to the room to hide behind the curtains with the others. For a time the street remained deserted and the parcel began to take on a distinctly sodden appearance. Then the Wee Fast Lady came pelting along, so named because she never walked but ran all the time. Our hearts jolted with hope, but she tore past the parcel like an express train and our hearts sank. Moments later a man came hurrying along, head bent against the driving rain. He came to the parcel, stopped, walked on a little way, came back and looked up at all the windows. We sucked in air and held it as he kicked the box into the gutter, a nonchalant whistle coming tunelessly from his lips. He took another hasty look at all the windows before he stooped, put the parcel inside his coat, and walked quickly away.

We hugged each other, then collapsed in hysterical laughter, Kirsty rolling about on the rocking chair, the rest of us prostrate on the floor.

'Let's do it again,' I choked.

Another parcel was made up and again placed temptingly on the pavement. This time we didn't have long to wait. A stout woman with a large shopping bag came along. Without hesitation she picked up the parcel, examined it openly, then, with an expression on her rain-washed countenance that said, 'Finder's keepers', popped it into her bag and went on her way.

This time we almost wet ourselves. It was so funny watching the different human reactions to our parcels we could have gone on with the prank for hours, had not Mam shouted, 'Tea time!'

In days to come, when we had nothing better to do, we made up our dummy parcels and got a terrific kick out of it all. Many of them found their way to the local Post Office, taken there by honest citizens, and we liked to imagine the postmistress's reaction as more and more of our mysterious parcels found their way into her hands. Not all our plans went off with such a hit. From time to time we were all keen to map out various schemes for making money to allow us to add a few luxuries to our lives, one of them being the delicious ice-cream cones from the 'tallies' at the corner. Pocket money was a hard commodity to come by, though we didn't question why other children got more than we did. We accepted the fact that we were poor and the only way to even the odds was to earn our own money.

At regular intervals we held jumble sales in the backcourts, gathering together tattered books and broken toys for the event. Kirsty, adept in the art of making tablet, shut herself into the scullery to stir delicious-smelling concoctions till her arms ached.

With great restraint we resisted sampling the results and to this day I can remember the ache of longing in my jaw while I wrapped that lovely tablet into squares of tissue paper.

Before one such sale we made all sorts of elaborate preparations. Kirsty made batch upon batch of tablet but when the great day arrived the rain was coming down in torrents. Our friends had looked forward to the sale because Kirsty's tablet was very popular and we had quite a squabble at the outside door.

'Sell yer tablet the noo,' we were urged and sticky pennies were proffered eagerly, but I had a mind to get rid of all our unwanted toys as well so we stalled for time by saying we would wait for an hour to see if the rain eased up.

A quick confab in the room followed. We were left to our own devices a lot, the room being regarded as our den, so we weren't too hesitant about finally deciding to hold the sale in the room and hastily arranged our stalls between the furniture. Laboriously I made out a large, colourful notice bearing the message, GRAND JUMBLE SALE, which I took to the front door to pin in a prominent position. Da had gone out for a few hours, our minds were easy, the sale would be over and the notice down before he came home.

Our cronies came up the lobby, poked at the stalls, most going away with the coveted tablet but leaving the rubbishy toys. My tongue wagged glibly as I tried to convince prospective customers that an armless doll or a legless panda was just the thing they needed to make their lives complete. The hours passed and our load of junk grew lighter.

Running through to the kitchen I said proudly to Mam, 'We've made enough to buy you a nice new apron.'

She sat at the fire, peacefully darning a great pile of socks, her smile lighting her face. 'Have you a lot of friends in? The door's been going like a bairn wi' too much castor oil.'

'We were selling our tablet,' I said breathlessly. 'It was too wet outside.'

'Och well,' she picked up a woolly sock, 'there's no' much you can do on a day like this, but don't let your father catch bairns tramping through the house.'

An imperative knock came on the door and I raced to open it. A large lady stood there, her face red with the exertion of climbing the stairs. 'Is this where the sale is?' she asked, edging her way into the lobby.

I gulped and stuttered, 'Yes, b – but . . .'

She stood in the lobby, dripping rain on the floor, and said, 'I heard aboot it jist a wee while ago. I hope I'm no' too late. Has all the best stuff been taken?' She peeked round the wall to the room. 'Where dae I go? Ben here?'

'Yes . . . no, it was there but . . .' I faltered and stopped.

Her bulldog expression grew determined and she

stomped past me into the room. She surveyed the furnishings, a calculating look coming over her swarthy features. 'It's no' up tae much,' she said with a shake of her head. 'I've seen better at a Sally Army hostel. How much is that chest of drawers?'

We stared aghast as she walked round our domain, looking at things with a professional air.

'It's not for sale,' I muttered, making frantic signs at Kirsty to air her seniority, but she didn't comprehend. I sidled up to her and hissed, 'Tell her it was only toys and sweeties! She just barged in the lobby. She thinks we're selling our *furniture!*'

Kirsty's face was crimson. '*You* tell her! It was your idea to have the sale in here.'

'Oh, that's a lie, we all wanted it in here!'

'Da will be in soon,' whispered a white-faced Alec.

At his words I flew to the door and took down the notice. When I got back the lady had decided she wanted my bed, the rocking chair, and the wardrobe.

'How much dae ye want for the lot?' she asked Kirsty. 'Mind, ye've a cheek tae sell it at a'. If it wis me I'd gie it away for nothing tae get rid o' it.'

At that moment the key turned in the door and I knew Da had come home.

Kirsty grew desperate and blurted out, 'They're not for sale, nothing here is! It was only toys and sweeties. It's only for children.'

A decidedly nasty look crept over the woman's red features. 'Whit dae ye mean?' she asked brusquely.

'There wis a notice on the door aboot a jumble sale and I wis told ye were sellin' yer furniture! Have I come a' this way in the rain for nothing?'

'Somebody's been kidding you on,' I quavered. 'We were only selling toys to our pals.'

'Oh! Oh, ho! Is that right? Well, we'll see aboot this! Where's yer mither?'

'Please go away,' begged Kirsty with tears in her eyes.

'Naw! I will nut! I want tae see yer mither!'

At that inopportune moment the door opened and Da popped his head round. 'Any o' you weans seen my tabaccy knife?' he asked then seeing the woman he said, 'Beg yer pardon,' and made to withdraw.

'Jist a meenit,' ordered the woman sharply. 'Are you the faither o' these weans?'

Da was immediately on the defensive at the woman's tone. 'Ay, whit of it?'

She treated him to an ominous glower. 'I'll tell ye whit! These weans o' yours have been puttin' notices on the door aboot a jumble sale in here. I came a' the way in the rain tae buy some stuff and wis told they wereny sellin'. Is that right?'

Da came further into the room and drew himself up to his full height, sparks flying from eyes that had turned steel-blue. 'Ay, that's right, they're only weans and they were playin' a game.'

We knew his protective attitude towards us was only for the benefit of the irate lady. Sparks would fly the minute she was gone. Her defences were crumbling rapidly in the face of his iron personality.

'Well,' she muttered in a grumbling voice, 'you should keep better control over them . . . that's a' I can say.'

'And you'd best get the hell out my house,' returned Da with frightening calm.

'Don't use that tone tae me, ye cheeky bugger,' she said ably, but she was already making tracks to the lobby. The door closed on her and we waited for the tirade to follow, but for once Da used a different approach. 'Get this mess cleared up,' he directed, 'then ye can all go tae bed. There'll be nae tea for any o' ye the night. Never let me catch ye up tae shenanigans like this again!'

Crestfallen, we set about clearing the room, wondering which was the worst kind of punishment, the knife edge of Da's tongue or the terrible fate of having to go hungry to bed.

We lay and watched the rain teeming down the window while our bellies rumbled incessantly in the gloomy silence.

Hours later, when the room was growing dark, Mam came quietly through bearing a tray heavy with steaming mugs of cocoa and thick slices of bread and jam.

'Sit up, the lot of you,' she said, trying to sound stern but unable to keep the warmth from her voice. 'I persuaded Pop to let you get something to eat, though you don't deserve it after a' the bother you caused. I thought you were only having friends in to buy your tablet. I never knew about the notice on the door. None o' you mentioned it to me.'

'We're sorry, Mam,' said Alec as we sipped the hot cocoa gratefully and wolfed into the bread.

'We won't do it again, Mam,' I promised. 'But we'll buy you a nice new apron to make up for being bad.'

In the dark her warm hand grasped mine and suddenly the world was all right again. She took the tray but paused at the door to say with a laugh, 'Och well, she didn't sound like a very nice wifie anyway. It served the bitch right to get sent packing.'

Treats and Tribulations

Sunday was always a quiet day in our house. There was a special, peaceful quality about it so that it could never be mistaken for a weekday.

Breakfast was a treat of fried eggs on toast, the latter made on a long fork held next to the fire. I enjoyed making the toast with the heat of the fire flushing my face and my imaginative eye seeing pictures in the leaping flames. I was inclined to dream a bit while I waited for the bread to brown and sometimes Da growled at me to hurry, but not on a Sunday with the aftermath of his Saturday drinking hanging like a thick curtain over all his sharp edges. We all took advantage of his mood. I was able to dally long over my toast-making, only called to earth by the second-in-command waiting impatiently with the butter.

Mam and Da shared the *Sunday Post* between them, Da's specs hanging on the end of his nose, his lips moving, while he devoured each item avidly. Mam relaxed in bed wearing her flowery cardigan, thoroughly enjoying her breakfast from a tray beautifully set with a china cup and saucer, a tiny milk jug and sugar bowl, and a glass dish full of butter which she spread with a little silver knife she had received in a present. She liked the good things, did Mam, and though she got so very few of them she was always fussy about her eating utensils. Hers had been a family of repute and the good manners and fastidiousness of her childhood adhered to her still.

We were contentedly quiet, able to relax over our breakfast because Da's attention was so taken up he paid little heed to anything else. When the meal was over there was the usual argument over the dishes but the minute I was free I grabbed the *Sunday Post* and raced downstairs to my 'reading room'. All the peace in the world was mine as I sat on the wooden toilet seat scanning each page quickly till I came to 'The Broons'. Sometimes the Toilet Paper Lady crept down to try the door but I gave no thought to her needs till I had finished my favourite articles. It became quite a contest between us to get to the cludge first on a Sunday morning, but if she pipped me to the post I unnerved her by bouncing a ball against the landing wall so that she made haste to leave the coast clear.

But to atone for my sins, the part of Sunday I didn't relish came all too quickly. We all had to get into our best clothes for our weekly visit to the Sunday school. Kirsty and I plaited each other's pigtails and Margaret's fair hair was brushed till it shone. Now that Ian was away from home so often Da had lost his passion for getting the boys' heads 'doon tae the wid', and

Alec's dark, wavy hair now sprouted thickly, though on Sundays it was watered down and put into a 'cow's lick'.

Armed with a penny each for the collection plate we set off to kirk, an establishment situated at the top of a long street. Kirsty marched resolutely into kirk every Sunday but on the odd occasion the rest of us played truant, spending our pennies in a little shop nearby, then retiring to the library till enough time had elapsed for us to go safely home.

One of my favourite pranks was to go into the kirk toilet with Alec and pounce out on the other children as they filed primly past. Pink cherubic faces looked down haughtily on such indiscretions and I was labelled as 'the girl who goes into toilets with boys'. Uncaringly I made faces at clean little girls and poked them in the ribs when they were being particularly anxious to please the teacher. If I was given a pretty marker for my bible as a reward for correctly answered questions, dark looks were thrown at me from the rest of the class which said plainer than words that a little horror like me didn't deserve anything.

Although Kirsty threatened to report our misdemeanours to our parents she never did, and our dear Mam never suspected that we were anything less than the good little souls she strived to create. Oh, how good it was to get out of our good clothes, which were usually someone else's best cast-offs, and return to the dubious recreation the backcourts had to offer!

On an occasional Sunday we were allowed to take the Govan ferry over to Partick to spend the afternoon in the Kelvingrove Park. Independence came quickly to tenement children, especially those who belonged to a large family. I loved the park with its wide open spaces and the magical lover's lane, dark and mysterious, smelling of earth, the tall, closely-knit trees breathing secrets into the sigh of the wind. We hid behind large trunks and giggled at young lovers strolling along, kissing and cuddling, locked away in their own little world.

When we had exhausted the pleasures of the park we popped into the nearby art galleries, going first to the cases that held the bones of prehistoric monsters. We also loved the glass jars which contained the innards of amphibious creatures, never tiring of staring goggle-eyed at gruesome curls of intestine and other viscera. The maze of glass-cased displays presented marvellous territory for games of hide-and-seek. We crept on tip-toe along polished floors and pounced on each other, disregarding the obvious annoyance of serious-faced adults.

On one occasion we lost Margaret. We hunted everywhere but she was nowhere to be seen.

'Maybe she fell into one of those old graves,' suggested Alec hopefully. He had been on rather bad terms with Margaret prior to losing her.

'Don't be silly,' I chided, but we hurried back to the room where the old graves had been reconstructed for public inspection. On the brown too-clean earth lay parched bones and crumbling skulls, together with urns filled with ashes of the dead. We forgot all about Margaret and stared afresh at the graves, our eyes delaying with morbid interest on the old bones. Just then the bell went for closing time and we looked at each other panic-stricken, not relishing the idea of being locked in with prehistoric monsters, stuffed jungle animals, and ancient skeletons. It was lovely to look at such things in the kindly light of day but how awful to spend the night with dead eyes watching you and the spirits of the long-departed haunting you at every turn. In such a place inanimate objects could be far more terrifying than things that moved. Even the suits of armour with black nothingness behind the visors had a certain eerie aspect about them. Da's pictures were benign in comparison.

Hastily we made our way outside and sat on the gallery steps, wondering what we were going to tell Mam. We couldn't very well go home minus our little sister but we consoled ourselves by telling each other how stupid she was to get lost.

'We have to drag her everywhere,' mumbled Alec.

'I know, she's too wee to be much use at anything,' I rejoined, though my mind was racing with the implications of the situation.

'She *is* stupid!' insisted Alec.

'Daft as a brush,' I agreed. Nevertheless, we were most relieved when the swing doors opened and an attendant came out leading a sobbing Margaret. She was a very angelic-looking child with her blue eyes and fair hair, and there were times when she used her charms to full advantage. She was using them now, looking up at the man with swimming blue eyes, and he had fallen for her – people did for Margaret. I, on the other hand, with my berry skin, green eyes and auburn hair, looked a regular little gypsy. I had no wiles to use to my advantage and my merry look incurred the suspicions of the adult world.

To make matters worse, the attendant was one who had admonished us earlier for sliding on the polished floors and when Margaret pointed at us, claiming us as her guardians, he glared at us with knitted brows. He had found Margaret wandering in the picture galleries where she had gone to look for us. Sternly he lectured us on our responsibilities and we received his words in respectful silence. Humbly we led Margaret away while he watched from the steps. At a safe distance I turned and yelled, 'Ya! Kilty cauld bum, big banana feet! Tickles a' the lassies and fa-arts in his seat!'

Breathless with laughter we grabbed Margaret's hands and ran for our lives to the safety of Mary's house situated a few streets away. Here we played with her baby daughter and were fortified with lemonade and biscuits before we set off on the long trek to the ferry. While waiting for the ferry to amble over, we threw stones into the oily waters of the Clyde and dared each other to climb down the greasy steps on the pier. Green patches of scum floated on the dirty water; pieces of debris bobbed on the black waves and we tried to catch them with long sticks. The little stretch of water between Govan and Partick was the only 'sea' we had ever known. The tang of salt water was an unknown element in our lives and it was as well I didn't know of the paradise that lay beyond the lower reaches of the Clyde or I would never have been content to live among streets again. Already the sky and green trees were precious, wonderful things to me, things to appreciate silently in moments of solitude, the patterns of clouds, the tracery of leafy branches. But beyond parks and gardens I knew nothing of the country surrounding Glasgow. None of us knew except Ian and he never spoke about it much.

On alternate Sundays, our house was full of visitors. Aunts came, bringing cousins, and the evenings were riotous with Mam telling endless funny stories. One aunt in particular laughed till the tears ran down her face and she and Mam seemed to do nothing else but take off their glasses to wipe their streaming eyes.

We were well behaved with visitors and even more so when we were visiting. Wild little monkeys in our world of play, polite little innocents in other people's houses, we stayed quieter than mice, listening respectfully while the grown-ups talked. This was really a great advantage. I learned a great deal just by keeping my ears pricked. When the talk got round to various aspects of procreation I listened extra hard while sang-froid sympathy was expressed for the poor souls who were 'away with it again'. Most of the facts of life were known to me by the time I was nine. Mam believed in calling a spade a spade. When I asked the so-called 'awkward' questions there were no evasive answers about storks and cabbages. Information was direct and I sifted it all away happily, marvelling at the miracle of life and at a God who had thought it all out so carefully.

God was spoken about freely in our house. Mam spoke about Him in the way she would speak about a dear friend, without embarrassment but with pride. Her belief in Him was almost childlike. She never went to church, yet I knew she thought far more about God than many people who did. She prayed for simple things, like health for her family and the strength to be able to look after us all no matter how difficult that was with so little money.

Yet, despite all, we did have some treats to brighten our lives, one of the most appreciated being a trip to the local cinema. Our parents had a habit of going every Friday and we had turn about going with them.

One such Friday it was decided to take Kirsty and myself, leaving eleven-year-old Alec in charge of Margaret. Kirsty and I were delighted and for once needed no prompting to wash up after tea. We got ready, Kirsty plaiting my hair and making sure I was tidy. Da changed into his good suit and Mam donned her best coat, a green tweed that brought out the colour of her eyes.

Off we set, bidding farewell to a rather sulky Alec into whose ears Da had poured a long list of safety precautions in the house. Kirsty and I skipped along and were at the cash desk waiting long before Mam and Da came in through the swing doors. At the sweet kiosk Mam bought her usual quarter-pound box of chocolates and we got threepence each to spend.

'It's a *horror* picture!' I breathed happily to Kirsty on the way into the darkened hall. It took some time for us all to get settled. Da was like a character straight out of a situation comedy. Off came his coat with a struggle and a few swear words. A flying sleeve slapped at a lady's hat, knocking it awry, the view of the people behind was blocked by his tall sturdy figure. A few disembodied remarks stirred among the ranks but eventually Da was settled to the accompaniment of a fervent 'Thank God' from a lady behind.

Now it was my turn to disrupt things. Eager to watch the horrible doings on the screen, I found my vision blocked by a huge lumpy head in front. Even with the aid of an uptilted seat I had to crane my neck from side to side in conjunction with the movements of the anonymous dome before me. Eventually I whispered to Mam; she in turn whispered to Da who rather grudgingly got up to change places with me. In doing so he had to take his coat with him and his spectacle case fell from his pocket. Kirsty had to grope about for it in the dark and when it was found and returned to the pocket we all had to stand up to allow Da to squeeze past. Clumsily he tripped over Mam's foot and landed on her lap, which gave me the chance to squeeze past the double barrier of their jutting knees. By this time we were decidedly out of favour with our fellow patrons and sounds of annoyance came from all sides.

For a time comparative peace reigned. Thunder and lightning crackled on the screen, infusing Frankenstein's monster with life. A period of breathtaking hush followed, during which Mam decided to open her chocolates. Engrossed in the picture, she removed the wrapping with a flourish, rolling it into a crackling ball that competed ably with the sound effects on the screen. The box was held in front of Da's nose. Liking soft centres, he never chanced pot luck, so he struck a match and peered into the box for what seemed eternity, his horny fingers fluttering uncertainly till the match went out and with a muttered 'Dammit' he shoved his hand into the box and chose at random. It was a toffee centre! After much loud chewing he calmly removed his teeth, struck another match to enable him to find the offending lump of toffee, extricated it from the plate, then ate it without the aid of his teeth which were only replaced when the sweet was finished.

We had come in during the latter half of the horror

picture but didn't mind, as we knew we would see the whole thing again after the showing of the supporting film.

At the interval we all got chocolate ices, Mam fastidiously spreading her hanky on her knee to catch the drips, Da making happy sucking noises. Mam was forever pulling him up for this habit, especially when he ate soup which he slurped from the spoon with lips shaped like a funnel.

'For heaven's sake, Pop,' Mam would scold, 'I've heard a coo drinking quieter out a pail. Anybody would think your lips were tacked up.' He was no better with his ice-cream and Mam threw him a few dark looks, but he was oblivious and sucked contentedly till he was finished. Out came his hanky, which he pummelled over his lips with enthusiasm. He blew his nose to produce a sound reminiscent of a fog-horn, then settled back to enjoy the big picture which was just coming on. He now wore spectacles for most things, after a bad accident while chopping wood when a large sliver had entered the eye with force. For almost a year he was back and forward to the eye hospital but eventually the eye had to be removed. Once over the horror of losing it he soon adapted to using an artificial one and was quite proud of how well the colour matched his remaining eye. It hurt him occasionally and caused a lot of watering, forcing him to remove it sometimes to give the eye tissues a rest.

Tonight the eye was giving him a lot of bother and

his hanky was out frequently wiping away the tears of irritation. Always proud of his appearance, he would never have entertained the idea of coming out minus his glass eye, no matter how much it hurt him to wear it. I was engrossed in the picture when his fiercely muttered words penetrated my consciousness. 'Christ, Evelyn,' he hissed at Mam, 'my e'en! It came oot wi' my hanky and dropped on the floor!'

I went hot with a horror that had nothing to do with the picture. Kirsty was squirming in her seat beside me, her face aghast. Poor, sensitive Kirsty! I could well imagine the agonies she was going through, visualizing the usherette flashing her torch about in search for Da's eye. But Da had no intention of employing the help of an usherette.

'Chris,' he whispered imperatively, 'I've dropped my e'en! Get doon and look for it!'

I didn't dare disobey but plucked up enough courage to say, 'Kirsty will need to help me.'

'Ay, the two o' ye can look for it,' he returned urgently.

Kirsty was almost crying as we grovelled among the debris of sweet papers and ice-cream wrappings on the floor.

'It's not here, Da,' I whispered.

'It must have rolled,' said Mam, *sotto voce*, keeping her eyes firmly fixed on the screen as if she had nothing at all to do with the situation.

A lot of tongue-clicking had been going on in the

row behind and now a lady's voice came out of the gloom in very forbidding tones. 'Whit the hell's goin' on here? It's a damt impossibility to concentrate on this picture wi' you lot playin' peep-bo in among the seats! I'm no' standin' it much longer. I paid good money tae get in here! I wish I'd brought my man . . . he'd have sorted ye oot!'

Da ignored her completely. 'Away ye go doon the rows, Chris,' he instructed urgently. 'Ask if anybody's seen my e'en. Some bugger might put a tackity boot on it.'

'Can we not wait till the picture's finished?' I asked in a trembling voice.

'No, we can't. Dae as ye're told and none o' yer cheek!'

'It's not fair,' I grumbled as I squeezed past knobbly knees and stood on several toes. I went down the dark passage, the giggle of nerves choking me as I put my question to several people. 'Have you seen my father's glass eye? It fell out his hanky and rolled.'

The giggles made everyone think I was kidding. 'Go away,' muttered an irate gentleman. 'Ye're just a damt wee upstart!'

But eventually I managed to engage the services of one or two people. The word got passed from row to row. 'This wee lassie's lookin' for her faither's glass eye. Can anybody see it?'

I was almost at the last row and nearing desperation when the eye was finally unearthed. 'Here it is . . .

doon here,' said a round-faced youth, staring with some awe at the object at his feet. It lay right way up, ghoulishly macabre. I pounced on it, feeling a slight revulsion as it nestled in my hot, sticky palm.

When I got back to my row Da leaned over and muttered, 'Take it tae the cludge and gie it a good wash, Chris. It'll be covered in germs.' Clicking my tongue loudly and feeling very hard done by I hurried to the ladies' toilet where I deposited the eye in a wash-basin and ran the tap over it. The force of the water made it go bouncing all over the place and I became engrossed in watching it spinning about, quite enjoying the dull chinking sound it made as it rolled against the porcelain. A lady came out of a toilet and parked herself at the basin next to mine. 'Can ye no' find a better place tae play wi' yer marbles?' she asked dryly. 'These toilets are no' playgrounds, ye know.'

'It's not a marble – it's a glass eye,' I said cheekily.

She peered closer into my basin. 'My God! So it is, ye dirty wee bugger! Take it oot o' there or I'll tell the manager!'

Hastily I made to depart but on reaching the door I turned and said solemnly, 'You'd better pull your knickers up before you go out of here!'

Her face blanched and she looked down at her ankles, whereupon I disappeared smartly before she realized I had only been pulling her leg.

At last I returned the eye to Da. Typically, he took it without a word of thanks and I settled down to watch what was left of the film. But the fun was not yet over. Da had no intention of facing the world without his eye so he inserted it into place in the dark cinema. He could have gone to the Gents' and sought the aid of a looking-glass, but he was of the stuff that disregarded such assistance.

The 'Queen' was played and we began to wander out of the hall and into the brightly lit foyer. The usherette was at the door and at first gave us no more than a cursory glance. Then her head swivelled round in a quick double-take. She was staring in disbelief at Da, her hand fluttering to her mouth which had fallen open.

With one accord we all turned to look at him and I at any rate felt that the monster we had recently been watching on the celluloid had stepped from the screen to come walking out of the cinema with us. Da's eye had taken on a new and hideous aspect. Most of the coloured iris was turned inwards and the white featureless globe that filled the eye socket was horrible to behold. It gave his face a sinister appearance made worse by the fact that he was grinning at the usherette and bidding her goodnight. 'Ye wonder who thinks these picters up,' he nodded, and the woman's face distinctly quivered. Da was always pleasant to people of passing acquaintance and they usually responded to his jocose remarks, but the usherette's reply came out in a series of inarticulate snorts.

I stood on tiptoes and whispered to my crimson-faced sister, 'He looks like Frankenstein's monster, doesn't he?'

'Oh, be quiet,' snapped Kirsty, holding her head high despite her embarrassment.

'John,' hissed Mam, 'your eye! It's in the wrong way.'

He looked at her in pop-eyed dismay, the smile fell from him, and he turned away to adjust the eye.

The usherette kept her face averted as we passed but being a keen observer of the human race I knew that she was watching us from the side of her eye, her whole being agog with natural curiosity though her entire demeanour suggested a dignified disinterest.

On the way home the funny side of the incident struck us.

'That wifie thought she'd seen a bloody ghost,' said Mam, throwing her head back and roaring with laughter.

Da chuckled. 'Ay, she turned a bit white, didn't she?'

'She thought you were a monster, Da,' I added, feeling the occasion safely warranted a cheeky comment.

He continued to poke fun at himself. 'If I'd taken my wallies oot she would have got a worse fright! Imagine nae teeth and a goggle eye!'

A giggle escaped from Kirsty who had been prone to a fit of the sulks for the last hour. It was difficult not to smile at the picture Da's words presented to the mind.

'I'll buy ye all a poke of chips for a treat,' he said benevolently. 'Kirsty, away you in and get them. Buy a bag tae divide between Alec and Maggie, they'll sulk if they don't get any.'

'Right, Da,' said Kirsty, her legs taking her quickly into the chip shop and mine following with a far greater zest than they had taken me in the quest for Da's glass eye.

Needles and Bedpans

I will never know why, how or when my lively, energetic little body became host to a rare disease that was to cause me many years of pain and inactivity. Health had always been a good companion of mine except for the usual childhood ailments. When Kirsty almost died of diphtheria at the age of ten and was so weak afterwards Mam had to wheel her round in a pushchair, I was sorry for my big sister but sublimely certain that nothing drastic would ever happen to me the way it did to Kirsty. These were the sort of things that always happened to other people. Such is the strength of human delimitation. If we didn't build our own little boundaries we simply wouldn't survive the mental strain.

I had just celebrated my tenth birthday when a bad attack of bronchitis kept me off school. Mam put me to bed in the warm kitchen and spoiled me thoroughly. This was much to my liking. Being confined to bed meant steaming bowls of broth and all sorts of tit-bits. Mam was a tireless nurse. She knew when we were acting and when we were really ill.

Coughing and spluttering, I lay in the bed recess, not too ill to enjoy my favourite storybooks and listening with half an ear to Mam and Da talking.

The bronchitis weakened my chest so much I was taken to a clinic where I lay in agonies of apprehension under a sun-ray lamp with my eyes covered by goggles. Soon after this I contracted conjunctivitis which had barely cleared up when I took an attack of jaundice which left me with an enlarged spleen and a total aversion to certain foods. I didn't really understand it all but Mam was kept busy taking me to doctors and clinics.

After a while I was sent back to school but my zest for life had gone. My legs ached with tiredness and I dragged myself listlessly round the house. At school I could barely pull one leg after the other. The other children thought it was all a pretence. I had always acted the clown and now they thought this was just another game so I was shoved and jostled and told to get moving.

During a routine medical examination the school nurse discovered I had shingles round my middle. I had endured the pain for days, not saying a word to anyone because I was afraid of all the strange things that had been happening to me. I dreaded the discovery of the painful little blisters because I harboured a secret fear of being sent to hospital.

'Lift your vest up, Christine,' said the nurse with calm detachment.

'It's attached to my knickers,' I told her, grimly holding on to the garment in question.

'Stop playing games,' she said, whipping up my vest

and spying my red band of spots immediately. 'You'll have to see your own doctor, Christine,' she told me kindly. 'I'll give you a note home to your mother. You can go home right away.'

Normally I would have shouted for joy at being let off lessons, but now I was afraid I had some awful disease. On the way home I swung my satchel half-heartedly and stared at the note in my hand, wondering whether to tear it up so that Mam wouldn't find out about my spots. Then I remembered, tonight was bath tub night. Out would come the big zinc tub, one after the other we would stand in it to get washed before the fire. My blisters were bound to be discovered so there was no point in tearing up the note.

Mam read it, then examined my belly. 'Och, Chris,' she chided gently. 'They're awful sore-looking. Why did you no' tell me about them?'

Hot tears sprang to my eyes. 'I think I've got a terrible trouble. I don't want to be sent to hospital.'

'Don't be silly, it's only shingles . . . though bairns like you don't usually get them. The doctor will give you something to clear them up.'

The doctor poked my belly, felt my spleen, and shook his head.

'She's always been a robust wee lass,' frowned Mam. 'Now she seems to be taking everything that comes along. It's no' like our Chris.'

After I had been given a good overhaul he took Mam aside and spoke to her quietly. I didn't know it then, but he was telling her he was going to arrange for me to go into hospital for observation.

Mam couldn't bring herself to tell me but one day a postcard popped into the lobby. Always eager to see what the postie had brought, I went to pick it up from the rough hair mat at the door. With incredulous eyes I stared at the card, then carried it through to the kitchen where Mam was making pancakes.

'Mam!' I exploded in panic. 'There's been a mistake! This card says I've to go to hospital! It's not true, is it, Mam? You won't let them take me away?'

She sat down heavily in her hard little chair to look at me with green eyes clouded with misery. 'Oh, Chris, my wee lamb,' she sighed. 'I should have told you but I didn't know how. Hospital's not the awful place you think, and it will only be for a wee while. They've got to find out what makes you so tired all the time.'

The world smashed round my ears. I couldn't believe the news and created quite a scene, screaming at Mam that I wouldn't go into hospital. I couldn't leave Mam and all the familiar things that meant security and love. I had never been inside a hospital in my life and the thought of what the doctors would do to me terrified my soul. I pleaded and argued with Mam till her dear face was flushed with worry.

'Please don't make me go,' I begged. 'They'll jag me and cut me up. I might never get out again!'

'Listen, Chris,' she said quietly. 'You don't have to go, I won't make you, my lamb, but I was always used to a healthy Chris, my own wee gypsy, never still for a minute. The doctors are clever, Chris, but you have to help too. You've got to be a brave bairn. If you're not then I really will think I've lost my Chris. You were always a daredevil, never afraid of anything. Da has always been proud of you for that. Do you want to let us both down?'

'No, Mam,' I sobbed. 'I'll go into hospital, but only for a wee while, not for keeps.'

She had won the battle but it was no triumph for her. 'Don't be silly,' she chided gently, 'as if I'd let them keep you forever. I would have no one to make me laugh the way you do.'

'Only for a week . . . or maybe two days,' I quavered bleakly.

The day Mam took me to the big general hospital I lost my voice and could do nothing but stare dumbly at people who spoke to me. As I watched my dear familiar mother walk away down the ward I wanted to die. I couldn't cry, tears were too superficial for the depths of my feelings. An efficient nurse got me into a cool white bed and I buried my head under the blankets, listening with a feeling of utter desolation to the strange sounds of my new world.

For days I refused to speak to anyone and lived only for the sight of my parents coming through the doors. They brought fruit and sweets but I had no appetite and told Mam in a sad little voice not to waste her precious money on such things. I knew what the sacrifice entailed and I couldn't bear to see her struggling to make ends meet. All I wanted was to be home with my brothers and sisters. My small hand lay in Mam's warm grasp, the strength of her burning into me. Da was gruff but kind and all at once I felt a great affection for him. In the past I had been too taken up with my youthful pursuits to spare time to analyse my feelings for him. Now I saw he was as much a part of my life as Mam was. He was dressed in his best suit, his watch chain sparkling, his back straight and proud. He fumbled for comforting words and I wanted to reach out and touch him. Long years of suppression kept me from doing so but I told him stoutly, 'Don't worry about me, Da. I'll be all right and I'll be home soon. Don't let any of the others sleep in my bed.'

But home was to be a very long way off. The hospital nights were long and I, who had slept like a log all my young life, now knew the awful experience of insomnia. Each night I lay and watched the night nurse sitting under a dim green light that threw eerie shadows on her face. Her eyes were lost in vast dark sockets, the blob of her nose was thrown into a shapeless lump. She looked sinister and I dreaded making the slightest noise lest she would search the beds for a wakeful patient. If my bed creaked I froze, my heart thumping in my throat, my whole being alive with the fear that she would come and give me an injection to make me sleep. All through childhood my mind had been fed on fantasies of hospital. Stories had been passed from other tenement children of hospital experiences where doctors and nurses perpetually injected people with huge hypodermics, of gorgon-like ward sisters who ruled nurses and patients with rods of steel. As the days went on and nothing very alarming happened, I began to relax a little and take some interest in my surroundings. I was the only child in a ward full of grown women and in the days ahead I was to get an education such as was never taught in any school. The children's wards were full, so in beside the adults I went. They were kind to me, trying to put me at ease despite my scowl and a total rejection of their attempts to include me in conversation. The ward sister was a large buxom woman with a forbidding expression but her voice was a soft lilting burr that had been nurtured far over the sea on the island of Lewis.

I gulped when I first saw her and thought, 'Wait till I tell Alec I've seen a *real* gorgon.'

Whenever she came near I quailed, expecting her to produce the biggest hypodermic of all. Instead she gave me picture books and smiled, an odd kind of smile that made me think her tight mouth was going to fray at the edges. She was pretty strict all round except with me and I soon grew to realize she had a soft spot for children.

I was a puzzle to the doctors. Not for me some straightforward disease like polio. X-rays became part of my life. Inevitably I had to have blood tests which were agony because my veins were difficult to find. Sometimes the needle had to be prodded around before my blood frothed colourfully into a syringe.

Something that had been bred in me wouldn't allow me to cry, no matter how painful the tests were. Injections were started, four times a day. Soon my hips were full of black and blue lumps which I showed proudly to Mam. 'I'm a human pin-cushion,' I stated grandly. I had heard the expression used by another patient and thought it sounded important, but Mam stared in horror. 'Chris, my poor wee lamb! How sore you must be!'

'I am, but I lie on my back so's not to hurt my lumps. The blood tests are the worst. I could cry really loud but I don't want anybody to think I'm a baby.'

'You're a brave wee gypsy,' whispered Mam, and her words made me all the more determined to keep up my front.

In time I was up and running about the ward, feeling important if the nurses allowed me to help make the beds and take round the cutlery trolleys.

Despite injections and exercise my limbs became progressively weaker and a biopsy was decided on.

'I'm to have an operation,' I told Mam, adding disgustedly, 'It's only to be a wee one, not a major operation – what does that mean, Mam? It sounds a lot better.'

'It means a really big operation, Chris.'

'Oh! Well, a wee one might be better.'

Before the operation I experienced for the first time

the awful mortification of an enema. I sat on the bedpan crying my eyes out and wouldn't look at the nurse who had performed the terrible deed for a full week afterwards. Pain I could bear but not humiliation. Two pieces of tissue were removed from my leg which helped the doctors to discover that I had an extremely rare disease, one that was so unusual that none of the medical textbooks gave it more than a passing mention. The calcium in my body had gone haywire. Far too much was being produced, the excess finding its way into my muscles and causing them to seize up. The doctors frowned over me and mumbled in technical jargon at the foot of my bed. Different types of treatment were tried, my injections were changed. There was no possible hope of my getting home for a long time to come.

Now quite at home in the ward, I observed my fellow patients with unending fascination. Many of them were old. Two had been sent from mental asylums for specialized medical treatment. They occupied special beds with high sides so that they couldn't climb out. One lady spent her entire day undressing herself and shouting, 'Mammy! Daddy!' over and over.

I watched her taking her clothes off, my eyes bulging, unable to believe the quantity of breast that hung in pendulous folds to her belly. I was really seeing life in the raw and my eyes almost fell from my head. But the novelty soon wore off. I felt sorry for the nurses who were kept busy running to cover the great breasts.

I took to shouting at Mrs Brown at regular ten-minute intervals. 'Mrs Brown, put your nightdress back on!'

At first she took no notice of my childish pipe but my perseverance began to seep through till the whole thing became like a game. The second she began to fumble at her attire she looked at me with vacant expectancy which was my cue to roar at her. Eventually she stopped removing her clothes and took instead to rocking herself back and forth all day – decidedly a more desirable occupation than the other.

The second lady spent her entire day ringing an imaginary till and talking to invisible customers. From her mumbled words I gathered she had run a post office in bygone days. I gulped and hoped the postmistress from our corner wouldn't suffer a similar fate through having to deal with my dummy parcels.

One of my special friends was an old lady known to everyone as Granny Walker. She was a gentle soul with snowy hair and twinkling faded blue eyes. The bond of understanding that can spring up between youth and age is an uncanny one, the pathway of life just beginning for one, the other nearing the road's end, with all the wisdom that only years of living can bring, offering so much to a good listener. For my age I was a very good listener and I grew to love Granny. I had never known my own grandmother and knew now what I had missed. Each morning I plumped Granny's pillows, combed her lovely soft hair, and carried her dentures to the bathroom to clean them carefully.

Two ancient ladies in the ward provided me with endless anecdotes to store up as future material to weave into my bedtime fables for Alec and Margaret. They were unmarried ladies, Miss Jolly having a long, doleful face like a bloodhound, Miss Trotter looking definitely like a small pink pig with her wrinkled snub nose and beady bright eyes. They spent the long days snarling at each other and finding fault with everything in general.

Miss Jolly was very envious of Miss Trotter's ring, which, inscribed with an affectionate message, was proof that once upon a time the little pink lady had known romance, but Miss Jolly was not going to let her think so for one moment.

'It's no wonder the mannie never married you,' she said one day to Miss Trotter. 'He was likely tired of yer girnin' face.'

Tears sprang to Miss Trotter's tiny eyes but she managed to utter a pig-like snort. 'Hmph, you've a cheek, ye auld spinster! At least I was engaged and I've my ring here to prove it!'

'Ay, weel, why keep it hidden away in yer locker? Wear it through yer nose! That way we can see it all the time!'

The ward was agog when one morning the ring went missing. Miss Trotter was beyond consoling, Miss Jolly looked positively triumphant. Accusations flew but despite the fact that the ring was found wedged in behind the drawer of the locker Miss Trotter was obviously convinced that her sworn enemy had a hand in causing her such anguish and vowed vengeance.

'Don't listen,' Granny Walker advised me as the two ladies cursed each other from here to hell, but I was thoroughly enjoying the quaint words and kept my ears well cocked.

The affair of the ring was forgotten till the day Miss Jolly's teeth went missing. She had a habit of wrapping them in a hanky and leaving them on top of her locker. They were kept for the sole purpose of masticating food, their decorative side holding no interest for Miss Jolly. Dinner was served and she reached for her teeth but they had disappeared. All hell was let loose. She dissolved into floods of tears and sobbed, 'It's that awful wifie! She's stolen my teeth because she thinks I hid her brass ring. It's her, I tell ye!'

That 'awful wifie' was of course Miss Trotter, who was looking as innocent as her pink, pig features would allow as she went on calmly eating her stew.

The nurses were harassed. It was bad enough having to cope with normal ward duties and the two battling ladies were a very trying addition to the usual routine.

'Miss Trotter,' said one nurse firmly, 'have you got Miss Jolly's teeth?'

'Naw, I have nut,' came the indignant answer. 'Who would want tae handle her damt wallies! They give me the wullies jist thinkin' aboot them!'

A week went by without a sign of Miss Jolly's teeth.

The nurses had hunted high and low but without success.

Not a word passed between the two spinster ladies and the ward was unusually quiet without their continual nagging. Miss Jolly huddled back in her pillows, the lower half of her face looking like a deflated balloon. She was huffed with the world in general and sat day after day, her hands folded over her stomach, her eyes staring grimly ahead.

Miss Trotter on the other hand was extremely bright, poking around the ward, prying into everyone else's business to such an extent that the whole ward began to wish she and Miss Jolly were on speaking terms again, if such a phrase could be applied to a continual verbal battle. At least the two had kept each other thoroughly occupied.

Even Mrs Brown forgot to rock when Miss Trotter hove into view and one day she said to no one in particular, 'That wifie's daft! Keep her away from me!' Whereupon the ex-postmistress stopped ringing her till for a moment to observe, 'They're *all* mad in here! I want to go home!' She nodded her head in dismay then said in a loud voice, 'Yes, dear, two stamps and a postal order . . . that will be three and sixpence.'

For my part I was extremely amused by the whole affair till the day Miss Jolly, still with folded hands and staring eyes, said dismally, 'It's that wee yin, that wee lassie! It's likely she that's hidden my teeth, she shouldny be in here wi' grown ups.'

I couldn't believe my ears. I had made an earnest search for the elusive teeth. In front of Miss Jolly's eyes I had made a great effort and got down on hands and knees to look under beds and lockers. Unable to defend myself against such an unfair accusation I burst into tears and hid my head under the blankets. Granny Walker came to my aid, putting her old arms round me, soothing me with comforting words. 'There, there, my wee pet,' she crooned. 'Take no heed of that spiteful woman. Here now, take a sweetie and dry your tears.'

Miss Trotter looked decidedly apprehensive after her enemy made the accusations against me and for the first time in days she spoke to Miss Jolly. 'Leave the wean alone, ye auld bitch,' she warned. 'It wasny her that took yer damt wallies!'

Miss Jolly sat up and stared like a hawk into Miss Trotter's face, and I realized then that the fly old bloodhound had only used me as a pawn to draw out the truth.

'Oh! – Oh, ho!' she gritted. 'And how dae *you* know that? Ye're as much as admitting it was *you* took my teeth!'

Miss Trotter didn't deign to reply but later that day her behaviour was rather odd. She wandered about the ward, peeping discreetly under beds and into corners.

'She's mad,' said the ex-postmistress. 'She should be locked up . . . yes dear, just sign here, please.'

Two days passed and Miss Trotter appeared to grow more and more anxious. Her peeping became less prudent. It was obvious she was searching desperately for something.

Mrs Brown became so disturbed by the continual prying that she resorted once more to her old habits and every ten minutes or so her breasts hung resplendently over the blankets and the nurses scurried frantically to cover them up.

'Be strict with her, Christine,' the staff nurse instructed me. Feeling very important I harangued Mrs Brown over and over. Miss Trotter peeped and searched, the nurses sighed, the ex-postmistress spoke with her invisible customers, Miss Jolly glared, and altogether the whole thing was like a bizarre pantomime.

The weather outside had been very hot and sultry and the windows had been open day and night for almost a week. Now a cold little breeze flurried inside and the elderly ladies protested vehemently. Nurse McLeod, a well-built young woman, went round banging windows shut with her usual vigour. One window proved difficult. Nurse McLeod pushed down with all her might and there was a distinct crunching sound. The nurse lifted the sash back up and from a corner of the frame pulled out a soiled little bundle.

'That's my hanky!' shrieked Miss Jolly. 'How did it get therc, I'd like to know!'

Nurse McLeod opened the hanky and a number of pink and white particles fell to the floor.

'My teeth!' yelled Miss Jolly, getting out of bed with amazing agility. She stared at the remains of her teeth lying on the polished floor, then bent to retrieve a piece of denture with one tooth attached, her sunken mouth falling open in horror.

Miss Trotter hopped hastily out of bed and made tracks for the bathroom. Miss Jolly followed, brandishing the broken denture and screaming, 'Whit did I tell ye? It was that bitch right enough! Come here, ye auld scunner, till I kill ye!'

Chaos reigned. Miss Trotter had shut herself into a cubicle and Miss Jolly thumped frenziedly at the door. 'Come oot o' there, ye coward! Come oot and let me kill ye!'

'I didn't mean it,' cried a petrified Miss Trotter. 'I only hid them for a joke, then forgot where I put them. I'm sorry, Jessie, really I am!'

'That's nothing to whit ye'll be when I get my hands on ye! Come oot this minute or I'll . . . I'll go tae yer locker and flush that brass ring o' yours doon the toilet tae be mixed wi' the rest o' the sewerage!'

'No,' whimpered Miss Trotter. 'Please don't touch my ring.'

The nurses had mustered forces and thronged into the bathroom. Mrs Brown rocked for a few moments then undressed herself with a flourish, her cry of 'Mammy! Daddy!' booming out with gusto. The ex-postmistress shut up shop and leaned back on her pillows, the rest of the ward clicked loud tongues, commiserated with each other, and from the comfort of their beds watched the proceedings with avid enjoyment.

'It's a shame about Miss Jolly's teeth,' I said to Granny Walker.

'Ach, never heed,' advised the old lady. 'You might not think so, my wee lamb, but the pair o' them are enjoying themselves. It's their way of brightening up their lives. They would be lost without each other, for they're just two lonely old bodies with nothing much to keep them going.'

Listening to the noises emitting from the bathroom, it was difficult to believe the wisdom of these words, but Granny Walker was wise in the ways of people. When Miss Trotter went home a week later Miss Jolly seemed to shrink into herself. The ward was so quiet that I selfishly wished the return of Miss Trotter. When she tottered in one day at visiting, going straight to Miss Jolly's bed, the ward held its breath. Even the visitors, well regaled with all the ploys, looked interested.

Miss Jolly seldom got visitors. For a moment she pretended not to see the little pink lady drawing up a chair to her bed. She remained hunched into her pillows, her lower lids lying on her cheeks, her long bloodhound face expressionless, but a look of expectant interest had come into her eyes.

They didn't say much to each other. Miss Jolly's hands remained folded on her lap and she stared straight ahead, but when Miss Trotter got up to go she said in a loud clear voice, 'Right, Aggie, I'll see ye next week. Bring me a poke o' mints tae sook. I canny eat much till I get my new teeth in.'

Eventually Miss Jolly too was allowed home and with her going the ward seemed very dull. But I still had Granny Walker to brighten my days. When she died, part of my childhood went with her. The ward was bright with morning sunshine when I sat up and cried, 'Good morning, Granny!'

There was no reply. I raised myself up to look towards the old lady's bed. There were curtains round it, solemn-faced nurses came and went, and I knew I would never hear Granny's voice again. The night before she had been the same as usual, kindly and bright, nothing to suggest that the angel of death would come to her in the night.

My young soul shrank from the truth. I couldn't believe that life could go so silently and swiftly. Granny had been old but she hadn't appeared ill enough to die.

When the shroud-draped trolley came to take her dear old body to the hospital morgue my heart beat swiftly with grief.

'Why do people have to die?' I asked Mam on her next visit. Her green eyes looked straight into mine. 'Because it's a part of life, Chris. Without death there would be no life because the world would get too crowded.' She smiled. 'There's more room in heaven.'

A sob of terror caught in my throat. '*You* won't die,

will you, Mam? Not till you're really old . . . at least a hundred . . . by that time I'll be old enough to die with you!'

'Chris, my wee lamb, don't talk like that,' she said softly. 'You have your whole life to live yet and I hope I'll be here to see you growing up.'

My feelings were very morose at this time and it was fortunate that a young girl of thirteen was admitted and her bed put next to mine. She was a lovely girl with thick auburn hair and a shy smile. Her name was Iona.

'What's wrong with you?' I asked, once we had both overcome our initial shyness.

'I've got someting wrong with my blood,' she volunteered readily.

'Oh! I've got something wrong with my bones. I think one day I won't be able to walk.'

Her lovely pale face became sad. 'That's a shame. Maybe God won't let it happen.'

'Do you think He'll let you get better?'

She nodded. 'Yes, I think I'm going to die.'

I stared. 'How will you get better if you're going to die?'

Her answer was full of childish faith. 'Because when people die they don't have any more pain. It must be better . . . mustn't it?'

I grew to love Iona. She never spoke of dying again. We spent our days laughing and getting into mischief. After two weeks of treatment she was sent home and

I was alone again. Renewed waves of homesickness swept over me in great tides of misery. I longed to see my brothers and sisters but the ward had strict rules. Children weren't allowed to visit. Once Mam brought them to a spot in the grounds where I could see them from my window. They stood in a solemn row, Margaret taller than I remembered, her fair hair shining in the sun, Alec, small and thin, his unruly curls tumbled by the lovely wind, Kirsty, quite grown-up-looking, her hair no longer in pigtails but cut in a neat bob with a fringe that I immediately envied. I waved till my arms ached, they waved back, but somehow I felt they were strangers, part of another world that was becoming a misty memory.

I had been in hospital five months, had watched other patients come and go in such a steady succession that I was beginning to fear that freedom was something I would never know again.

It was high summer, the trees waved thick green fronds in the breeze, the sky held the blue mists of heat in its entirety. I longed to smell the sweet air, to inhale the cool night winds heavy with the scent of new-mown grass. The summer smells filtered faintly in through the windows but it wasn't enough for me. I wanted to embrace the sky, to roll on the earth, to feel the whip of the wind tugging my hair. I pined for the bitter-sweet familiarity of family life. Beds were objects to be hated. I thought if I ever got out of hospital I would never want to sleep in a bed again.

Never having been a child for gazing into mirrors, I wasn't aware of my changed appearance till one day I got a glimpse of myself in the long mirror of the physiotherapy department, which I attended twice a week for wax baths and exercise. At first I didn't recognize myself and stood staring solemnly at a thin little sprite with a white face. My hair cascaded in auburn waves down my back to my waist. The nurses were forever admiring it and brushing it but I had never even bothered to look at it. Seeing its beauty I no longer wanted Kirsty's bobbed locks. I stared at myself, feeling I was looking at a stranger, a cruel shadow who was mocking me because the frail shell of my body had, by a chance in a million, contracted a rare disease for which there was no known cure.

After spending nine weary months in hospital I was sent home. It was Christmas time and the wards sparkled with trees and tinsel. Now that the long-awaited departure from my cocooned world had arrived, I felt oddly apprehensive. Vaguely I remembered the grey tenements of home. In comparison, the hospital seemed suddenly bright and gay. The trees, sparkling with a thousand lights, were a big attraction to a little girl who had known only home-made decorations strung across a dingy room.

Secretly I knew I was clinging to straws. I knew that life consisted of so much more than superficial things like Christmas trees and tinsel. I had grown up a lot in hospital. It was difficult to remain a child in a world of life and death, pain and boredom. My quick restless spirit had been stifled in an existence that demanded a great deal of patience.

So I went home. The doctors could do nothing for me except wait for the next stage of my illness to show itself.

Gods and Gorgons

It was strange and frightening coming home to the tenements. Grey chimneys loomed into grey skies. The streets looked dirty after the clean white world of hospital. Suddenly I dreaded meeting my brothers and sisters again. I who had been the leader in mischievous games now felt an intruder into a world that had become foreign to me.

I arrived at the close in an ambulance and children who had once been my playmates stared at me with the blank, round-eyed detachment of strangers. They were gathered in a tight curious knot near the ambulance, snot-nosed, grimy faced, giggling, whispering, all belonging to each other and shutting me out.

As I walked slowly out of the ambulance and into the close I realized that my life would never be quite the same again. The thought came swifly into my brain. At ten years and nine months old I felt adult, wise, and very sad.

I walked into our tiny kitchen. It was warm and steamy because it was Monday and washing was in progress. My throat tightened as I looked around, seeing the big black range gleaming with its Sunday polish, the bed recesses with Mam's bedspreads glowing with rich colours, the two old chairs shining with a new coat of varnish, and the table in the corner boasting a new table-cloth because Ian was home and working, bringing in some extra money. On the dresser, among the clutter of knick-knacks, sat a tiny tree, its needles a rich green, the light from the window glancing off the home-made silver baubles and paperchains. And there was Mam, her hands damp from scrubbing clothes, but warm and gentle as they reached out for mine to lead me further into the room. It was all so familiar, yet my long separation had warped my memories of it, my longings had bloated it out of all recognition so that when I was faced with the reality I wanted to shut my eyes to the obvious poverty that lurked in every corner.

'C'mon, lamb.' Mam's eyes were strangely misty. 'I'll make you a nice cup of tea. I bought a wee cake specially for you. It's so good to see you home, it's never been the same hoosie since you went away.'

The love in her voice swept away all my doubts and my heart began to sing. Da sat in his chair, great clouds of smoke billowing from his pipe and all at once the smell of it was the sweetest smell on earth.

'It's great to be home, Mam,' I said, lowering my tired body into the old rocking chair brought from the room specially for me.

'Do you like the tree?' Mam asked hesitantly. 'It's no' as grand as the ones in the hospital but Kirsty and

Ian saved up to buy it for you and Alec and Maggie made the decorations.'

I looked anew at the tiny green tree. The fresh smell of its needles brought the pine forest into the kitchen, balls of silver paper and squinty stars nestled among the branches. It was a symbol of love, an evergreen offering of welcome from a family who were happy to have me home.

'It's the nicest tree in the world,' I said huskily.

'Ach, it'll jist make a mess,' said Da gruffly, yet he hastened to replace a star that had fallen from a branch.

'Are the others at school?' I asked, still feeling like a rather polite guest.

'Ay, but they'll no' be long,' said Da, pouring tea, hot and strong the way he always made it. 'That Maggie had better be in sharp for I want her tae get me some tabaccy. Auld Carmichael's gettin' wandered, she shuts her shop whenever she feels like it now.'

I choked into my tea with laughter. In a few moments my father had swept away my feelings of unreality. Here was my world, here were my people, speaking a language I understood. There were no pretensions, no false glossy words, no fuss.

The others tumbled in from school and work. All through tea an unnatural politeness prevailed between them and me. Table accoutrements were pushed respectfully in my direction. It had been so long since I had sat round a family table I felt embarrassed. The others eyed me covertly and I felt shut out. Because of his long spells away from home, Ian was even more a stranger than the rest. He and Da didn't get on. They never had really, but in the past Da always had the upper hand. Ian at nearly seventeen was asserting his manhood and he and Da niggled at each other in their struggle to maintain what each thought was his place in the home. After tea Ian disappeared smartly on some manly pursuit, and the usual war cries filled the kitchen.

'It's *your* turn for the dishes!' Alec yelled at Margaret.

'I did them last night *and* I went for Da's tobacco earlier!'

Kirsty, her smile sweetly deceptive, turned to me. 'It's *your* turn, Chris. You haven't done them for months.'

That did it. Margaret and Alec swung round on me. 'Yes!' they cried in unison. 'It's your turn, Chris!' and Margaret added quickly, 'You've missed a lot of turns! You should really do them for a year!'

I was truly home. I looked at Kirsty but her eyes were downcast, a smile curved her mouth, and I knew no words were needed to thank my big sister for bringing me into the squabbling bosom of the family once more.

When bedtime came and I was feeling somewhat strange in my little iron bed the feeling was soon dispelled when Margaret's voice came out of the darkness. 'Tell us a story, Chris.'

'Yes, tell us a few.' Alec's words tumbled from the bed recess. 'Could you tell us that one about the Christmas star that fell out of the sky?'

'I might,' I taunted, feeling my old power returning.

Muted cries of encouragement filled the room.

'Be quiet, you lot!' roared Da.

'I'll tell you a new one,' I whispered, 'about an old lady who died and became a Christmas angel.'

'Oh yes,' hissed Margaret, the tears already in her voice for an old lady who became an angel at Christmas. So I wove Granny Walker into my tales and even convinced myself that far above the stars of infinity she flew on silver wings, her spirit as bright as the spirit of Christmas itself.

That year a most longed-for gift came to us in a fateful and unusual way. Da had never allowed us to have animals though we tried everything to get him to unbend. Once he had relented and told us we could have a cat but it had to be orange. He had been a keen Orangeman in his day and his choice of colours for various things had been greatly influenced by this fact.

We had searched high and low for an orange cat and eventually found a big battle-scarred tom with one eye. He was dirty, smelly and bossy but his faults were tempered by his charming affection. Da took to him immediately, loudly proclaiming his virtues, but I suspected that he saw the one-eyed cat as a kindred spirit, one with the same disability as himself and with the same single-minded ideas for gaining the upper hand.

We had Tom for a week, a week in which he reigned supreme in our household. In the afternoons he cat-napped on a comfortable bed and slept on top of the oven in the evenings. But he had obviously been a Casanova of the cat world and went off on the tiles one night never to return.

To console ourselves we fed and nursed every stray in the district. The neighbours complained bitterly about the smell of cats in the close till the strength of their united voices couldn't be ignored by Mam, who loved animals and closed her eyes to a lot of our cat-caring activities.

We tried to forget about having a pet till that eve of Christmas 1953 when a quick light rap came on the door. A scruffy small boy stood on the landing and in his arms snuggled a beautiful black and white kitten. The boy's story was long and involved but we managed to discover that he had rescued the kitten from a crowd of boys in the act of throwing it from a stairhead window. Our patronage towards animals was known to the boy and he hoped earnestly we would give the kitten a home, thus justifying his act of heroism.

'My Mammy's oot workin' and canny keep cats or dugs,' he concluded with a dismal sniff. 'And my faither's oan night shift and would skelp my lugs if I go hame wi' a cat in the middle o' the day.'

Mam simply couldn't refuse the plea. She took the kitten in her arms, gave the boy sixpence, and shut the door.

‘What about Da?’ we asked, joy and apprehension struggling within us.

‘Leave him to me,’ she said firmly.

We swarmed round her into the kitchen. ‘Will you look at what I’ve got, Pop?’ she said, stroking the kitten who was purring fit to burst.

Da looked up from his paper and his expression grew fierce. ‘There’s no bloody cats coming in here!’ he snarled.

‘It’s already in,’ said Mam, with that special quiet determination she had. ‘It’ll be good for the bairns to have an animal . . . you never give them anything at Christmas . . . let the kitten be a present.’

He stood up, his one eye blazing with fury. We all took up strategic positions round Mam. Da’s fists bunched but the expected blast of rage didn’t come. He lowered himself back into his chair and muttered, ‘I’ll kick the brute if it gets in my road . . . I tell ye that!’ He glared at me, ‘Chris, you see and keep it away from me.’

It was his way of telling me the kitten was mine. My weak legs trembled with relief.

We spent Christmas mopping up little puddles and keeping the kitten out of Da’s road, but it showed a marked preference for his knee. Each time it approached he swiped it away.

‘I’ll strangle ye, ye skunk!’ was Da’s loving cry of encouragement. He took every opportunity to indicate that the cat was nothing but a nuisance, yet one day I caught him with it on his knee, his rough fingers tickling the little white throat, its purrs filling the kitchen.

'Ye damt wee puffer, ye,' chuckled Da affectionately, thereby christening the kitten with the most suitable name so far suggested.

So Puffer came and stayed, proving her worth in Da's eyes by turning out to be an excellent mouser.

'Jist as well it earns its keep,' Da growled sullenly, slipping Puffer a tit-bit when he thought no one was looking. Puffer was a feline aristocrat, aloof, mysterious, intelligent, more cunning than Da himself. She made the most of any opportunity to make herself an agreeable cat in the eyes of this soft-hearted tyrant who was a mass of contradictions. In the end her dignified perseverance won and she soon earned a comfortable and assured place in the family circle.

When the magic of Christmas was over I settled uneasily into a new way of life. I was sent to a special school which taught physically and mentally handicapped children. In my mind, the very word 'special' set it apart, labelled it as different. I wanted to be tomboy Christine Fraser, wilder and stronger than any boy, with legs that could carry me up trees and over walls.

I hated the school with a hate different from that I had felt for my old school. That had been a dislike of discipline and certain academic subjects. This was a dislike of an alien world, a disbelief that I was a disabled child, the same as all the others. I wasn't the same, I knew that, but no one else seemed to know it because the teachers treated me the same as the rest. It was wrong of them to lump me in and I resented them. Even though I had lost a lot of schooling I was well ahead of the others in my class. Some were older than me yet I felt they were babies. I was too young then to realize that the majority of the children had probably spent more time in hospital than out.

Epileptic fits were quite a common occurrence in the classroom. The teachers were cool-headed, efficient, kind and, most important of all, they were patient. My youth and ignorance blinded me to these facts. I hated it all, from the little grey bus that took me to and from school to the pink, rhubarb-tasting medicine we all lined up for each day after dinner.

It was a world where I stood on the fringe, an onlooker, a stranger. I looked at poor little twisted limbs and felt horror, I stared at calipers and crutches and felt frightened. That wasn't going to happen to me; I couldn't be looking at effigies of my future self. From my old school came gifts of fruit and sweets. Strict, fussy little Miss Black was the benefactress and all at once she loomed in my mind as an angel. I forgot all about her leather tawse, her flying skirt, her long bloomers. In my mind's eye she was benign and smiling. I wanted to be back under her regime once more, to know I was normal and devilish enough to be on the receiving end of her sharp tongue. I cried into the fruit, I pushed aside the sweets. They were lovely gifts but the kind of things only given to the sick. I didn't want to be thought of as anything other than untidy little me, a rogue, an urchin.

Shamefully, I took my feelings out on Mam, alternating between temper tantrums and moods of resentment.

A few months went by. I was in poor health. My pent-up excess of calcium sought an escape and my body broke out in torturous sores. It was possible to squeeze calcium from the smaller sores, like toothpaste from a tube. Pot-holes in my knees and the base of my spine were agony to touch. Mam was a wonderful nurse. Three times a day she dressed the open wounds while I cried with pain. I was attending the out-patients department of the hospital and after one such visit it was decided that I would have to be admitted once more to hospital.

'I can look after her, doctor,' said Mam, loath to part with me though I meant so much work for her.

'No, Mrs Fraser,' he told her. 'Christine needs to be under our supervision and there are one or two new drugs we'd like to try.'

So I returned to my old ward, the medical ward for adults. It was easier to put me there because the doctors were familiar with my case. I wasn't really sorry to go back to hospital. I was very tired and no longer ran about the ward. My muscles were so weak I could barely lift my head from my pillow. The sight of food made me feel sick. Injections of cortisone restored my appetite though the drug's side effects puffed up my face and caused my heart to race. I was tried on a calcium-free diet, then a salt-free diet. When the doctor told me I was being put on a diet that included charcoal, I didn't know what he meant and smiled dumbly. I always smiled like an idiot at the doctors because they were objects to be treated with awe, not people but objects who patted your hands, smiled, told you how wonderful you were, how brave you had to be.

When the doctors made their morning rounds it was a revered hour. A pin could have been heard to drop. One deaf old lady gave me many private giggles because of her sweet oblivion to all conventions. Unfailingly she needed a bedpan during doctors' rounds. What a crime that was! For anyone to need a mundane thing like a bedpan while the Gods were on their rounds. Disgraceful!

Little student nurses scurried to draw curtains round Granny Mitchell's bed and a discreetly covered bedpan made a discreet journey from slounge to Granny, who grunted and fussed while the nurses shooed at her to be quiet. But Granny Mitchell was an incorrigible old dear. No one could stop the rumblings that issued from behind the screens; ably amplified by the metal bedpan, they ripped the silence of the ward apart. Doctors listening for heartbeats were confused. They frowned, and Sister McQuarry's lips became a thin line. In her I had met my real-life gorgon. Unlike my Hebridean Sister she didn't look like a gorgon. She was young and slim with a pretty face, but her lips were tight and her blue eyes cold. She didn't have to speak twice to send the nurses running at her bidding. A flush crept over her neck to her face when she was angry. Unlike my fat old Hebridean Sister, she didn't appear to like children, and I knew my tender years would earn no concessions from her whatsoever.

She was clinically clean, from her starched white head-square to her neat, medium-heeled black shoes. No wrinkles marred the seat of her skirt and I often wondered if she ever sat down.

One day Doctor Masters approached my bed, patted my hand, and asked how I was feeling. I gave him my unfailing answer, 'Fine, thank you.' I think if I was dying I would still have said that.

'Good girl, Christine, good girl,' he approved, and I felt like a small puppy who was taking to a rigid training routine quite admirably. He mumbled to Sister McQuarry and she whipped the screens round my bed. My starched hospital gown was drawn up to my chin and I lay passively while my famous spleen was prodded and my limbs worked this way and that. Again my belly was poked, stimulating my bladder. But I had learned a lot of control since my illness. Granny was rumbling uncaringly from behind her curtains and my stifled giggle came out in a snort.

'Did that hurt, Christine?' asked the doctor, his fingers fluttering above my navel. Sister McQuarry glared behind his back and I hastened to assure him, 'I'm fine, thank you.'

'Good girl,' he approved again. 'You're coming along nicely but we are going to try you out with something new.'

That was when he told me about the charcoal, but I didn't take in the full import of his words till a nurse came to my bed the next morning bearing a plateful of shrivelled black morsels. 'Specially for you,' she beamed cheerfully.

'I can't eat that!' I said in horror.

'It's part of your treatment,' she said firmly, leaving the plate on my locker.

'I'll get poisoned,' I told my fellow patients tearfully.

'Get it down!' they cried with all the sadistic fervour I had thought was only common to Da. 'Get the boilers stoked.'

I crunched the hideous stuff, washing it down with the watery orange juice from the jug on my locker. After a few days I was sick of the whole business but felt too ill to protest or care much about anything. It was difficult for me to sit upright in bed. Even with pillows stuffed round my back I lolled to one side, unable to stay put. The pillows were eventually taken away and I spent my days lying flat on my back. I ate and drank in this position. The nurses were often too busy to help me at mealtimes. I rejected such aids as feeding cups, which I felt were too related to helplessness. Flat on my back, I refused to depend on anyone and devised my own methods for getting food and drink past my lips. Da's seed was in me, there was no doubt of that. I had inherited his tenacity, which was my most valuable asset at this critical stage in my life.

Day merged into day, doctors came and went but could find no ready cure for my illness. I was too young and terrified to question the Gods. Mam did, of course, but they couldn't tell her very much. One night she went off determinedly to seek out Sister McQuarry. I saw them in the corridor, Mam small-looking beside the tall, coldly detached figure of Sister McQuarry.

When Mam came back her eyes were very shiny. She looked odd, the way she looked when she wanted to cry but was holding it back.

'What's wrong, Mam?' I asked in panic. 'What did she say?'

'A lot of nonsense. I don't like that wifie very much. She's a cold fish. Don't worry, lamb, I'll make sure they get you up out of this bed.'

That which had upset Mam so badly wasn't known to me till years later. That night Sister McQuarry had told her, quite unemotionally, that my bones would just crumble away, I would deteriorate quite quickly, and if the calcium didn't stop its rampage through my body it would get into vital organs like heart and kidneys, all of which didn't make for a very bright future if a future at all.

But at the time I knew nothing of this. Despite my

weakness I was full of hope. Every time the doctors came I waited with bated breath for them to reach my bed. The great decision on whether a patient remained 'inside' or went home lay with the real Gods, the professors who came once a week on their hushed rounds. Next to them the ordinary doctors were like real human beings with no pedestals to make them seem ten feet tall.

The fuss on the great day was unbelievable. An army of cleaners arrived at daybreak. Beds were tidied to such a state of neatness they seemed to be much more important than the mere humans who occupied them. All unnecessary items were packed into lockers with the concession of a magazine or book that one could pretend to read till the Gods came to your bed.

Bladders and bowels were squeezed dry as the great hour approached. Little ladies hastened to add discreet smudges of rouge and lipstick to pale faces in an effort to deceive the Gods into thinking that they were bursting with good health. Granny Mitchell was enthroned so long on a bedpan she was eventually driven to roar out despairingly, 'I canny pee any more, nurse!', bringing to mind the realization that even the Granny Mitchells of the world had their limitations.

During that stay in hospital I had a young companion of my own age in the next bed to mine. We were at the giggly stage and the sombre procedure of preparing for the Gods only served to make us more merry.

Two days after Mam's talk with Sister McQuarry the Great Gods came on their weekly visit to our ward. The swing doors opened and they crowded in, a silver-haired professor, another with beetling brows straying over horn-rimmed specs, three 'ordinary' doctors with my own Doctor Masters in their midst . . . and, horror of horrors, a large entourage of students with shuffling feet and pimply faces. My rare disease evoked a great deal of interest from the professors who took a real delight in showing me off to the students. There was a general move to the first bed. The patients on the left-hand side of the door were the lucky ones. They were the first to be visited. Those at the top of the ward weren't so bad either, though much sweat and frustration had to be endured before the Gods reached them. The poor souls on the right hand side of the door were the worst off. An hour could pass before their turn came. By that time they might be bursting for a bedpan and with the dinner trolley having arrived in the kitchen the smell of cabbage would be in full competition with perfume and talcum powder.

My bed was near the top of the ward on the left so I only had half an hour to tremble before the Gods descended on me.

The ward was hushed. Only the mumble of the medics' voices broke the deathly silence. The students shuffled. One or two dared to smirk at each other. The rows of neat white beds might have contained corpses, so quiet was everyone.

Granny Mitchell sat up amidst the folds of a voluminous pink bed jacket. Her bright little eyes took in the scene with interest. She was not in the least awed by the Great Gods and spoke to them at length about her two cats, her gas bills, the state of her bowels, the effect the hospital food had on her delicate digestion. But she had a long wait before the Great Gods reached her bed that day, because she had been moved to the other side of the ward. Her bright eyes grew heavy, her head lolled, tiny snorts and puffs escaped her lips.

Mary began to giggle. 'Granny's teeth are coming out,' she gasped.

'*Shh!*' I warned in agony, because the Gods were only five beds away. But Mary, blonde, blue eyes shining in a cheeky face, had started and couldn't stop. 'Look at Granny,' she persisted.

I glanced over and sure enough the old lady's teeth were hanging over her sagging lips. A sucked-in breath snatched the precarious teeth back in. Moments later they were expelled once more on to her lower lip.

The bubbles of mirth rose inside me and I choked them back desperately. Mary was already lying on her back with her hands clapped over her mouth.

The Great Gods were intently examining some X-ray plates and the students were gaping at them with a great show of interest. The silver-haired professor shot a question at one bespectacled young man who reddened and seemed lost for words. For a moment there was complete silence. The entire ward was suspended in deathly quiet. Granny Mitchell moved slightly and a great ripple of flatulence tore from beneath her blankets to go belting round the ward like a military tattoo. The old lady opened her eyes, muttered a weary, 'Beg pardon,' and went immediately back to sleep.

Well, that did it! I squirmed and screeched with mirth. Mary shrieked and clutched her stomach. The Great Gods tore their eyes from the X-ray plates to look forbiddingly in our direction. A slow flush crept over Sister McQuarry's neck and she whispered to a little student nurse who broke from the group and scurried towards us. The trolley containing the ward's case histories was parked at the foot of a bed. The little nurse caught her foot on a castor and down she sprawled, skirt to the waist to reveal brief yellow knickers and rows of suspenders.

The students all looked long and hard at what was obviously a rare sight in the middle of a working day. Delight fought with sympathy in their expressions. One or two made a discreet rush forward. The Gods were making a great show with the X-ray plates but took sneaky looks at the yellow knickers and the suspenders. The professor with the horn-rimmed glasses seemed particularly confused by the sight, his eyes swivelling rapidly between the network of bones on the plate and the rather shapely little legs on the floor.

Through my laughter I saw with dismay that the nurse had a hole on the heel of her stocking in a spot normally covered by a shoe. But the shoe had come half-way off, the hole gaped like a crater on the moon. I felt really sorry for the nurse but the sight did nothing to sober myself or the hysterical Mary. We shrieked louder, Sister McQuarry's face sparkled with rage, the little nurse went running off in tears, and Granny Mitchell woke herself with an extra loud foghorn of a snore.

I knew Sister McQuarry would never forgive either Mary or me but I didn't care. In a way I was glad to be getting back at her for all the snide remarks she had doled out to me. After all, what could she really do to me for laughing before the Gods? I couldn't be put into any more of a prison than the one I was already in. She couldn't hit me. She could glare and make tight-lipped sounds of disapproval but these I had already endured without any lasting damage.

When the Gods finally came to my bed it took all my control not to laugh in their faces, but this was now a nervous reaction.

'This young lady seems in fine fettle,' commented the beetling-browed professor, throwing me a grimace that was meant to be a smile. 'How do you feel . . . er . . .' He consulted my chart. 'Christine? Better – eh?'

'I'm fine, thank you.' I said the unfailing words quickly, then something dared me to add, 'But I'd like to get up. I'm sore lying in bed all the time.'

I held my breath at my audacity.

'Hmm.' He frowned, then went into a huddle with

the other medics. The students stood aimlessly, obviously discomfited by Mary's occasional snigger.

Sister McQuarry received whispered instructions and the screens were whipped round my bed. One by one the students lined up to prod my belly, marvel at the little holes in my limbs where calcium came out like toothpaste, and generally look me over. It was awful lying there, everything exposed, cold fingers squeezing with ineffectual gentleness or poking avidly till I felt my bladder contents would erupt and my spleen rupture at any moment. Sister McQuarry was enjoying my discomfiture with a tight-lipped satisfaction. The students were put through the usual third degree but it was a very brief affair. Whether the laughter of two little girls and Granny's indifference to protocol had knocked concentration out I'll never know, but my gown was placed carelessly over my skinny little body and the looks on the Gods' faces suggested my case held no more interest for them at the moment. Sister McQuarry looked disappointed but whipped the screens away from my bed. Everyone was drifting away, not a word was said to me. Then, like an afterthought, Doctor Masters looked back and said briefly, 'You can get up tomorrow, Christine. We'll see about getting those legs of yours moving.'

I was so overwhelmed I couldn't answer. I had lain for almost two months in bed; now suddenly I was to be allowed up and I wondered vaguely if Sister McQuarry had said anything to the doctors about Mam's talk with her.

Mary was being told she was to get home and she was bouncing on her bed with joy. Her news made mine miserably insignificant, and my first feelings of happiness dispersed rapidly.

Without Mary the days were long and dreary but Annie, the young ward maid, brightened my daytime hours. Every morning she breezed into the ward, the click-clack of her polisher keeping time with her merry humming. If anyone needed a bedpan and no nurse was available, Annie flew into the slounge calling gaily, 'Right! Bums ahoy and mum's the word!'

With help I could now sit up and every morning before breakfast Annie got behind my bed to haul me upright. I had discovered on getting up that the strength in my legs had almost gone. It was impossible for me to get out of bed by myself, but Annie swung my legs round and while I swayed dizzily on the edge of the bed she put on my slippers and enclosed my little body in a big hospital dressing gown. My legs wobbled like jelly but Annie supported me on the way to the toilet and walked me about the ward. Unable to straighten my legs, I felt like a disabled banana as Annie half-dragged, half-carried me on these expeditions.

Because of the rarity of my trouble I had several little trips to other parts of the building so that Doctor

Masters could show me off to various colleagues. For long hours I lay on hard couches in little ante-rooms while the doctors came and went. Sometimes I think they forgot all about me because on one occasion a guilt-ridden nurse came to my rescue at nearly midnight to take me back to my ward. I grew resigned to the waiting but with nothing to read, nothing to do, I was forced to control the wild activity my body had once known and channel it instead into my fertile mind, locking each character, each situation away to be sorted out later at leisure, because I had decided that one day I was going to be a writer, one so utterly brilliant the world would know about me. My notebook was my brain. I couldn't very well sit with pencil and paper while doctors pressed cold hands against my belly. How could I lie writing in detached splendour while my limbs were folded about like bits of spaghetti and I was asked to touch my nose with my eyes shut or push my feet against a doctor's hands to see how much strength remained in them?

One day Doctor Masters asked me if I would go to a students' conference which was to be held in one of the big Glasgow teaching hospitals. 'You're a special case, Christine,' he beamed flatteringly. 'You don't have to go but just think how much help you'll be to students who have to study so many subjects to become doctors. You'll be a challenge to them.'

Having experienced the amazing theories put forth by dozens of students on my case, I didn't share the doctor's optimism, but I fell for the flattery bit. I felt grown-up, important, and looked forward to the big day with all the zest of someone going on a big outing. I had been in hospital five months and never been further than the physiotherapy department, so I was quietly excited at the prospect of a trip in the ambulance. When the trolley came to take me from the ward I felt special. Pretending I was going home, I shouted my farewells to everyone. During the journey I caught glimpses of trees and chimneytops from the small clear slits of the ambulance windows. I felt I was looking at another planet, a world I had grown away from in the confined sphere of hospital.

Breathlessly I waited for the ambulance to stop so that I might experience the wonderful feel of air on my face. For one brief, glorious minute the wind caressed my face and ruffled my hair. The August sky was blue above the hospital towers, the smell of life was all around me. While the ambulance attendants joked with me and I smiled, deep inside I cried for freedom.

I was indoors all too soon, through corridors to a large hall with beds all round the walls. A curtained-off cubicle swallowed me up and I was left to stare at a large jar on the bedside locker. I picked it up to examine it, trying to make some sense of the technical jargon written on the label, and very soon I realized I was staring at beautifully preserved bits of my leg floating around in a clear fluid. I gaped with morbid interest, my mind going back to the Glasgow Art Galleries and my careless perusal of preserved viscera.

The curtains fluttered and a doctor came in, quite a human grin lighting his face. 'I see you've found yourself!' he said, taking the jar and putting it back on the locker. 'Interesting . . . eh?'

I smiled stupidly, my usual awe engulfing me. The doctors were so clinically clean in their white coats with stethoscopes hanging from the pockets. I was still to learn that behind every white coat lurked a human being with the same hopes, the same fears as everyone else. All morning the students popped in to tap my limbs with little hammers and ask me questions. I felt at ease with these young men who had not yet acquired the finesse and distant manner of their seniors.

After lunch the qualified doctors asked the students questions. Faces reddened, voices faltered. Many of the young men took refuge behind my glass jar and its gory contents, heads nodding, fingers pointing at the label with what appeared to be unerring understanding. Several Great Gods were present. They were holding my X-ray plates to the light and I stared at them along with the students, amazed at what was inside my skin. The Great Gods mumbled, pointing out various structures to the students who nodded knowingly. One young man had his nicotine-stained fingers crossed behind his back and I smiled, wondering if, like me, he thought that each stick-like bone looked the same.

When the day was over the Gods thanked me, one stretched his lips into a surprisingly warm smile, another patted my head absently, a junior God winked, then they moved off in a tight group murmuring in medics' language and I knew the limelight was over. It was time to go back to my own hospital.

Kirsty was a regular visitor. She brought paper bags filled with home-made potato crisps. She must have spent patient hours slicing potatoes into wafer-thin particles to cook in the chip pan, but she always came faithfully armed with greasy bags filled with the tit-bit. I think if it hadn't been for Kirsty's crisps I wouldn't have stayed alive because I ate very little hospital fare.

Kirsty was a working girl now and to my eleven-year-old mind she looked grown-up, with an air of mystery when she spoke of dances and parties where boys had been present.

'I wish I could go to a party,' I told her one day as I delved into the bag she had brought. 'It must be lovely . . . mind you, I'd rather be out in the fresh air to smell the grass and the flowers in the park.'

Tears sprang to Kirsty's eyes. 'There's no flowers now, Chris,' she said quietly. 'It's winter and cold outside. Maybe you'll be home for Christmas. It's only four weeks now . . .'

'Is it?' I said bleakly. 'I lose track of time in here. All the days are the same, Kirsty. It always feels the same too . . . never cold or warm like outside. Have I really missed a whole summer? I wonder if there was a lot of catties in the park this year. I wish I had some in here to keep me company.'

Kirsty shuddered. 'Don't talk about creepies, Chris. I always hated the way you used to keep them under your pillow.' She giggled. 'Still, it was a scream that day you told me they all came marching out of the cludge.'

'I know! D'you remember the look on old Toilet Paper's face?' I moved restlessly. 'Och, I wish I was home to play some tricks on her again . . . the only thing is . . . I might not be able to walk up and down stairs . . . I won't be able to torment the Toilet Paper Lady again!'

The full realization struck me and I stared aghast at Kirsty.

'You will, you will!' she said passionately. 'The doctors told Mam you were a lot better. She's going to ask them if you can get home for Christmas. I'm going to buy you a nice jumper to come home in.'

'I'd rather have a white mouse,' I said dismally.

'Puffer would kill it,' said Kirsty happily. 'You're better with something to wear.'

The bell went and she rose to go, bending down and dropping a kiss on my cheek in a really grown-up manner. I watched till she was out of sight then with a sigh I put the crisps into my locker, my appetite suddenly gone.

I didn't get home for Christmas. The ward sparkled with tinsel and fairy lights. I remembered a tiny tree that smelt of green pinewoods, decorated with squinty stars, and I put my head under the blankets and wept.

A week before Christmas the old lady next to me was moved and an empty bed placed next to mine.

'A new patient's coming in, Christine,' the staff nurse explained. 'She's only a few years older than you and we thought you would like someone young beside you. You can spend Christmas together.'

'Oh,' I said without interest.

The nurse paused. 'She's also very ill, Christine. You're such a cheeky wee thing, we thought you could maybe brighten her days.'

The enormity of such a responsibility did nothing to cheer my heavy heart. I sighed and wished I was away from illness, pain, and death.

A trolley came into the ward but I could see nothing under the huddle of blankets. The usual bustle of settling in a new patient followed, then the curtains were pulled back and I looked to see Iona's lovely, pale face nestling against the pillows.

'*Iona!*' I gasped.

'*Chris!*' she cried. 'Oh, I've thought a lot about you.'

She looked very ill, with a transparency about her skin that showed the delicate network of veins on her temples. She was also very weak, barely able to lift her head from the pillows. I knew instinctively that quite soon she was going to die. The shadow of death was on her face.

'I've thought about you too,' I whispered.

'Can you walk still?' she asked eagerly.

'Only a little, my legs won't hold me up. I won't get home for Christmas.'

'That's great, Chris,' she said then laughed. 'That sounds selfish but it only means I'm glad you'll be here to keep me company. Will you tell me some stories, the kind you tell your brothers and sisters at Christmas?'

I nodded. 'Yes, I'll tell you stories, Iona, lovely stories about Christmas angels and magic stars . . . but you might not like them . . . you're about the same age as my sister, Kirsty, and she's a bit grown up for my stories.'

'I'll like them, Chris,' she said softly. 'Oh, I'm glad I got into the big ward! They wanted to put me into one of the side rooms but I don't want to be alone when I die.'

She said the words so frankly they took away the apprehensions that were building up inside myself. On seeing how ill she looked, I'd felt that the responsibility of being companion to a dying girl was too great. Now I felt honoured, grateful to God for letting me know a girl like Iona.

'Aren't you . . . afraid?' I asked hesitantly.

'More sorry, really. I love so many people and when I go they'll be sad and I don't want that. I love the world too, things like the wind and the sun. Do you think about things like that?'

My breath caught in a tear but I nodded. 'I love them. I wish sometimes I could get up and run out of here into the air . . . just to *smell* it! I don't know how you *can't* be afraid though. I'd be terrified.'

To my shame I burst into tears and dived under the blankets.

'Don't cry, Chris,' said Iona anxiously. 'I don't want anyone to cry because then I *will* be afraid. Don't cry again . . . promise?'

'Okay,' I said shakily, knowing in days to come I would cry inside myself a thousand times for a girl called Iona who was young and lovely and not afraid to die.

Iona's condition grew steadily worse. I sat by her bed every night, combing her thick auburn hair and telling her my tales of castles with turrets that reached to the sky to touch the stars, of fairies that came alive on Christmas trees, of angels with silver wings that came to visit loved ones on the night of Christmas.

Sometimes Iona fell asleep before my stories were finished but on the night before the Eve of Christmas she said cheerily, 'I'm going to be one of your Christmas angels, Chris. I'll watch over you . . . I promise . . . do you believe me?'

A strange urgency had crept into her tones. I felt afraid and too inexperienced to cope with a dying girl seeking reassurances about a world that existed after life.

'You do believe me, Chris?' she said again, and a slight hint of anger sharpened her voice.

The ward was hushed, the tinsel and decorations sparkled. At the top of the ward the deep green needles of the tree were splashed with the rainbow colours of the fairy lights. Outside the hospital the night sky glittered with a million stars, but one star twinkled brighter, so big it dominated the black sky. I looked at it and thought of home where all the preparations for the festive season would be in full swing. I thought of Mam who'd had 'flu and hadn't been able to visit me for nearly a fortnight but was coming to see me tomorrow. I thought of myself, a born tomboy now losing the power of legs that had once carried me on effortless wings. All the strength of me was now locked inside, an unleashed wild spirit curling and churning till I thought I could scream with frustration. I had wondered why God picked me out of millions of children to be the receiver of a rare disease which no one knew how to treat. I hadn't spoken to anyone about my feelings but inside I was angry with God for letting such a thing happen. Now I looked at the star and Mam's voice came to me, talking about God in her childlike way. Life hadn't been very kind to Mam, yet she never questioned God's existence. A young girl called Iona was going to be robbed of her life, yet her belief in God was strong though now her time was drawing near she was seeking reassurance that her life wasn't going to be spent in vain. It was up to me to give her the help she needed.

'I believe you, Iona,' I said brightly. 'In fact . . . I *know* you're going to become an angel, and you won't just have silver wings, yours will be gold because you believe so much in God.'

She lay back on the pillows. ‘Do you know how I got my name, Chris?’

‘No . . . it’s a funny kind of name . . . funny beautiful. I don’t know anyone else called Iona.’

‘Well, Iona’s an island where a lot of Christian people go on things called pilgrimages. My Mum and Dad went there before I was born. They wanted children but weren’t able to have any. Mum told Dad that if they ever had a daughter she would be called Iona because while they were there they prayed for children. I was born two years later and Mum said I was a gift from God, though I was so wild when I was little she said I had a devil in me.’ She laughed. ‘I used to do awful things and played with boys all the time.’

I giggled, relieved to know that a girl with such a firm faith had achieved it all even with a devil inside her like I had. ‘I’m glad to hear that, because I was beginning to think you were an angel while you were still here on earth.’

‘You must be joking, Chris! I’ve been a rotten little bitch sometimes! I’m no angel.’

The next day Mam, Da, Kirsty and the others all came to see me, bearing gifts. Ian shuffled in awkwardly and went away early, leaving behind an enormous sweet shop. Margaret and Alec beamed at me shyly, then squabbled over the grapes I gave them. Mary came marching in, her dear familiar face all smiles. I hadn’t seen her for weeks because she had so far to travel, and the joy I felt at her entrance brought tears to my eyes.

Visitors milled to overflowing, the spirit of Christmas was everywhere. Everyone began to intermingle and lonely old ladies with no one to care for them were inundated with other people's visitors.

When Mary came in, Da went outside for a smoke and Mam went to see Iona whose vast amount of friends and relatives had thinned out a little. When Mam came back I asked, 'What did you talk about? You didn't say anything about . . . about . . .'

'Don't be afraid to say the word, Chris,' said Mam softly. 'It happens to us all in time. She's so young though, and what a bonnie lass. She did nothing but speak about you. She thinks a lot o' you, Chris.'

'I wish she didn't,' I said gruffly. 'All I do is tell her stupid stories. She must be sick of me.'

'I wish you were home to tell us some stories, Chris,' said Alec. 'Christmas won't be the same this year.'

'It'll be horrible in here,' I said bleakly. 'You have to stop talking early and you're not allowed to hang up a stocking.'

'We're hanging ours up,' said Alec eagerly.

'Well, you can fill them yourselves,' said Kirsty, who had in recent years taken over quite a few roles from Mam, whose health was never great now.

'That would be daft!' cried Margaret. 'How can we fill our own stockings . . . ?'

'Be quiet or I'll skin ye,' said Da in a fierce hiss, and we all glowered at him behind his back.

The bell went and I felt a lump rising in my throat. My family were going, leaving me to spend my first Christmas away from home. The mound of parcels on the bed did nothing to cheer me. The nurses descended to make beds and I sulked at them, unable to respond to their cheery comments.

Then I looked over at Iona. Her eyes were sunk into her thin face and a flush high on her cheekbones only served to heighten the pallor of her skin. Yet she was smiling. Her parents had been allowed to stay on, and she was talking to them animatedly. Her mother got up and came over to my bed, laying down a gaily wrapped parcel. 'I hope you like this,' said the tall, grey-eyed woman. 'I think the colour will suit those merry green eyes of yours.'

I couldn't find words but I didn't need any. The woman laid her hand on my arm. 'Iona's been telling us about your castles and your Christmas angels. You've made her time here a happy one. Her father and myself are grateful to you, Chris.'

'Thanks,' I whispered. Iona looked over at me and smiled. It was the last time I saw her smiling. Soon after she sank into a coma, the curtains were placed round her bed, and her parents were with her all evening.

Sometime in the half-real world of dawn she died without ever regaining consciousness. In my dreaming mind I was aware of nurses and doctors, the shadowy figures of relatives, and the bowed, hushed grief of two people who had received a gift from God only to lose it again. Then I thought of Iona's faith and knew that they hadn't lost that gift. They had parted with it only for a little time and one day they would meet again a small angel with golden wings who hadn't been afraid to die.

When the silent hours of night were over the bed beside me was empty, as if Iona had never been there.

A nurse came over to me. In her hands was a tiny doll with silver wings. A note pinned to it read: 'I'll put in for my gold ones when I get up there.'

'Iona made it for you,' said the nurse. 'She was going to give it to you today but . . . her mother asked me to give it to you instead . . . Merry Christmas, Christine.'

I took the little doll. Hot tears burned my eyes but I knew that Iona lived, somewhere she lived and watched. The thought took some of my grief away. I was able to open the parcel her mother had given me. Inside was a pale green nightdress such as I had never owned before. At home it had been vests and knickers, in hospital starched shapeless nightgowns because Mam couldn't afford to buy me fancy bedwear. I wore the fine new nightdress for my visitors, feeling for the first time a vanity about my appearance that I had never known before. I began to look in mirrors but didn't really like what I saw. Except for my tumbling mass of hair and my grey-green eyes I thought myself very unattractive. My bones seemed to stick up everywhere. When one of the hefty physiotherapists told me rather unkindly she could use my knobbly shoulders for coat hangers, I scowled but knew she was right. I was barely four stone, but my general health had improved and I began to feel young again. The calcium in my body had abated a good deal and I no longer suffered agonies with sores. With the returning of my health the old restless urges to escape hospital came to the fore and the Gods agreed to let me go.

Immobility inside hospital hadn't worried me greatly but once home, knowing the great wide world lay down a flight of stairs, my position became unbearable.

Kirsty and Ian were out at work, Alec and Margaret at school, so I was pretty lonely. Mam was my constant companion. I became closer to her in spirit than to any human being I had ever known. We talked for long hours, reminiscing over the days of my early childhood and all the escapades I had come through. If I started to feel sorry for myself she turned the conversation to lighter things till I laughed at myself. Never pampering, never rushing to my aid, she made me self-reliant and independent. Sometimes I felt angry at her because I felt she made me do too much. With a basin on my knee I peeled the potatoes every day. I still had to take my turn with the dishes, even though it meant they were handed to me from the scullery to dry. I polished the cutlery, cleaned the shoes, all without moving from the big rocking chair because now I could barely walk at all.

Now I know Mam suffered, watching me do things that were often a great effort. She stifled her natural impulses to help me because her mother-love was greater than her need to satisfy her own instincts. She was preparing me for a future where my greatest asset would be my independence.

Da had mellowed with the years and was reasonably tolerant towards me, but I could feel the tension in him when he watched me struggling with the simplest task. He never mentioned my disability, but I knew it was agony for him to watch me. I had been one of his strongest children and I sensed the sadness in him for the loss of that strength. Yet I knew he was proud of me for other reasons. From the time I learned to write I had spent a good deal of time jotting down little verses and stories. Now I went into it with a vengeance. Mam bought me jotters and pencils. I spent all my free time writing and she read out the results to Da. He listened, one hand over his glass eye in a characteristic gesture.

'Ay, that's no' bad,' he would say gruffly. For someone like Da that was an uproarious burst of approval.

Getting round the house was difficult. Da carried me to my bed at night and into the kitchen each morning, which was quite a feat for a man of seventy-eight. But I was like thistledown in his wiry arms, he never showed any sign of strain.

The journey to the cludge was out of the question for me. The Toilet Paper Lady was having her greatest reign of peace since my arrival into the world.

Mam solved the problem in her usual frank manner. 'You'll have to use the chanty, Chris,' she told me cheerfully.

'But I can't!' I wailed. 'It's okay for a pee, but . . . nothing else.'

Mam just laughed. 'Most of my life, Chris, I've changed dirty nappies. Emptying a chanty's nothing to me. None of us know what we'll have to do to help each other before we're through, so think nothing o' it. Don't keep it in or you'll get constipated, then I'll have to give you syrup of figs.'

I shrieked with laughter. Mam and her syrup of figs was a standing family joke. If any of us looked pale, out came the bottle. Once she had been administering the syrup to a constipated Margaret and Alec had grumbled because he thought he was missing some sort of treat so Mam had given him some laxative too. For two days he spent his time running to the cludge and he never asked for syrup of figs again.

The days of high summer came round, making me more restless than ever. I sat at the kitchen window watching the children in the backcourts, longing to join in their games but even more to be out in the fresh air, to feel the sun and the wind. I stretched my arms to the sun till they became a startling golden brown in contrast to my face. The flowers in Da's window box were a source of joy to me and I appreciated these gifts from God more than I had ever done before. Gifts from God! They were many and varied, but the right to walk had been taken from me and I wondered in my straightforward way what God was going to do about it.

Blue Horizons

The idea of a wheelchair never occurred to any of us till one fateful day Mam was telling a neighbour about the long hours of boredom I spent in the house.

'Why not a wheelchair?' said the neighbour. 'My nephew's disabled and my sister has just got a new chair for him. The old one's there for anyone who wants it.'

So I came by my first chair. It was a huge affair with a wickerwork seat. I was so small and thin I disappeared into it but it had wheels and I had no qualms about using it. It was my passport to the world. On a day of blue skies Da carried me downstairs and Mam took me on my first outing to the Elder Park. Gulping in great breaths of warm fragrant air, I imagined that I would never want anything more than these walks to the park with my dear Mam. But I was wrong. I was only twelve years old and my youthful energy smouldered inside like an unexploded firecracker. I longed for excitement and Mam understood. One day she told Alec and Margaret that they were to take me for 'a nice walk'. Their eyes gleamed because they had long itched to get their hands on my chair. Under their careless guidance it became a miniature tank. They battered me up and down pavements, my bones and teeth rattled but I laughed to the skies with joy. I wasn't a sedate little invalid any longer. My health had improved greatly. The unleashing of my wild spirit was like taking the cork out of a champagne bottle.

We wandered round Govan, poking into the trees in the park for caterpillars. I was too young to be embarrassed when passers-by looked first at my chair, then at my legs to see what evidence manifested such a premature halt to activity. I stared back and stuck out my tongue uncaringly. It was later, in my adolescent years, that I experienced the terrible embarrassment wrought in me by the curious.

We were quick to discover that my chair made a great hiding place for ill-gotten gains. At weekends we went along to the plots, small patches of cultivated land. From my chair I watched while the daring Margaret helped herself to fat sticks of rhubarb which she stuffed down the sides of my wickerwork seat. Sometimes we were spotted and Alec and Margaret would each grab a handle of my chair to zoom me in and out of dusty potholes away from the danger zone.

People looked askance at such rough treatment but I loved every minute of the outings. They were beneficial in many ways, the most important being that I was never allowed to feel sick or helpless. Mam smiled when she saw the sparkle back in my eyes. 'These walks are doing you good, Chris,' she approved.

Had she witnessed the wheelchair acrobatics I was subjected to she might never have allowed me out for another 'walk' again. Margaret was the daredevil. She was very partial to excitement and loved taking me to the top of a hilly street to sit on the steps of my chair and with both her feet in the air we whizzed downwards, the squeal of my tyres at the bottom causing a few heads to turn in horror. At other times both Alec and Margaret put one foot each on the crossbars of the chair and used it as a sort of scooter, turning me round corners on one wheel.

Much to my disgust, the question of my education came to the fore. I would have been quite happy never to look at another schoolbook again, but it was not to be. Tuition at home was decided on and a tutor came to me twice a week. I had lost a lot of schooling but didn't really care and I made the fact quite plain to my poor teacher. I learned very little in the paltry time allotted to me by the education authorities, but if I had put my mind to it I could have learned a lot more. I felt I knew all that was necessary to get me through life. My own intelligence and quick wit were my allies. I knew how to read, spell, and write. With my ambition to be an author already fixed in my mind, I felt I was armed with all I needed to know to enable me to carry out my ambition. Words were magic to me. I could weave them into so many creations.

I spent a great deal of time reading, soaking up

information like a sponge. I knew I learned far more in this manner than I ever did under the guidance of my tutor.

I had been out of hospital six months when a visitor came to our little house especially to see me. She was a Girl Guide Captain and had acquired my name from the almoner at the hospital. She wanted to know if I would be interested in joining a branch of Guides for disabled youngsters. I sat in the rocking chair overcome with shyness as she explained things to Mam. My months in hospital had left me with a total lack of self-confidence. So long as I was with my own people I was full of self-assurance, but meetings with strangers were a nightmare in which I just could not bring myself to converse in an intelligent manner. I was beginning to experience the disquieting sensation of having a member of my family act as my interpreter.

Mam welcomed the Guide Captain's proposition. It was a way out of my restricted life to wider horizons. Another door opened into my world the day I joined the 1st Glasgow Post Guide Company. At first it meant corresponding with other disabled girls and receiving magazines full of Guiding activities.

After a while parties and picnics were arranged, the Guiders providing or organizing the transport. It became quite a commonplace occurrence for sleek cars to draw up at the close. I was unable to help my feelings of superiority when I looked from the car at the mobs of untidy children staring in wide-eyed awe at the proceedings. I told myself they were not so fortunate as I, even as I remembered that once I had been one of them and would give a lot to belong to their world again. But there was no turning back, my life was going ahead in the way fate had decreed.

Meetings were held in a Guide hall and our Company was formed into patrols. I became a keen Guide and my pride in my uniform was tremendous. Everything that could be polished gleamed. Every spare penny I possessed was saved to buy knives and compasses to fit on the rings of my belt. When summer came we were told that arrangements for our first camp had been completed. The news was received with great enthusiasm. The countryside was an unknown element to me, camping a thing I had only read about, and I looked forward to going away with an impatience that could barely be contained.

My one regret was that I couldn't share the holiday with my wonderful Mam. She had never had a holiday in all the years of her two marriages and her health had suffered in consequence. Occasionally she spoke of getting to her beloved Aberdeenshire for 'a wee change', but though two of the family were out working there was never quite enough for the luxury of a holiday.

The day before I left for camp I watched her going about her work. I noticed the weary droop of her shoulders. With a catch in my throat I saw the silver glints in her bright hair.

She sat down on her uncomfortable little chair and taking a sock from her workbasket began to darn it neatly. Even when she was sitting her work-worn hands were never at rest. Silently I observed her and a wave of remorse washed over me. 'I can't go away and leave you!' I burst out. 'You're the one who needs a holiday!'

She looked at me with eyes full of love. 'Don't be silly, Chris. You go and enjoy yourself. You need a wee change after all you've come through and it must be dreary for a young lass to sit at home all day . . . don't think I'm not wise to it. My turn will come . . . one of these days. Just write me a wee letter when you're away and I'll know you're thinking of me.'

Before I left the following day she slipped two crumpled pound notes into my hand. 'I'm sorry it's not more, lamb,' she said apologetically. 'I managed to put a pound aside from Ian's wages and a pound from the gas rebate I got last week . . . weesht now – I can manage.'

A lump came to my throat and I felt I would choke with the hurt of it. 'Thanks, Mam,' I croaked. The door went. 'I'll write, Mam, I'll write . . .'

Her face was at the room window, watching me being helped into the ambulance that was to take our Company to Linlithgow. I looked up and waved. Her hand fluttered cheerily in response but I thought she looked lost and very alone. The engine revved up and we drove away from my familiar street. I felt desolate and resentful of the cheery chatter inside the vehicle.

Many miles went by before I could respond to the

lighthearted gaiety of the others. I was a sulky little creature in those days, prone to fits of moodiness. I liked a lot of solitude, which was perhaps unusual for someone of my years, but I had spent a lot of my childhood in a prison of sorts which may have had something to do with my temperament. However, I couldn't stay solemn for long that happy day in the company of the other Guides. Some of them had very bad disabilities, yet they were such happy girls.

It was a glorious June day with the sun shining hotly from an azure sky. I glimpsed trees flashing past and an excitement grew in me at the realization I was on my way to the country at last. Inevitably we began to sing the miles away. I had learned many new songs during my months with the Guides. Singing and Guiding seemed to go hand in hand and no gathering was complete without our repertoire of songs.

Our Guiders were a cheery lot. We had a Brown Owl in our midst, affectionately known as Wullie. She was quaintly sturdy with pink skin and merry brown eyes. Mrs Winters was a Guide Commissioner, tall and dark, her conversation liberally sprinkled with schoolboy slang, a result of having two sons at boarding school in England. Miss Morrison, our Captain, was thin and quiet, a bit of a listener like myself. The remainder of the Guiders had gone ahead of us to get everything ready. They were at the gate of a big field when we arrived, ready to welcome us and take us immediately to long tables outside a marquee.

The camp was in an estate belonging to titled people who were connected with the Guide movement. Fields of buttercup and clover stretched away for miles, groves of oak and sycamore were outlined against the blue sky, bees droned lazily amongst the wild flowers, and birds twittered cheerily from the trees. I stared and sniffed and fell in love with God's green acre, knowing it was a love affair that would remain in me forever.

My first meal in the open was an experience of fleeting impressions. Greedily I stored each one away so that I would remember them always. How natural it seemed to eat under the roof of the sky. What better music than that of the birds and the soft hush of the wind stirring long grasses? The fragrance of sweet warm air and meadow flowers was a drug to my senses.

Then . . . suddenly another picture floated to the surface of my mind, that of the dingy grey tenements and the smell of the middens on a warm day such as this. What a comparison I made then. I thought of Mam, her warm hand touching mine, pressing the money of sacrifice upon me, her silver head bent over her darning, her face at the window, all alone in that moment of waving me goodbye. My heart leapt with love for her and the hot upsurge of tears filled my eyes. I was sad and happy at the same time and I could hardly bear the depths of my emotions on that first day of camp. Although I sat at the table I was not wholly there. The chatter round me faded as I fought to contain all my feelings. I knew now of the world that lay outside of towns, yet knowing didn't make me happy because I knew there would always be an unrest in me now. When I was back home in the tenements I would feel the craving that a lover might feel knowing that a love is unobtainable.

'C'mon, Chris, you're not eating,' said a very everyday voice at my elbow, and I came back from my reverie to stare rather shakily at my untouched plate.

The meal over, we got things into our sleeping quarters, which consisted of a sturdy wooden hut for those unfit to sleep under canvas and several tents for the Guides who were more able. My heart bubbled with joy because I had a certificate from the doctor that pronounced me well enough to come into the second category.

The sinking sun had turned the sky into a rose-pink as we sat round the fire drinking cocoa. Everyone was chattering but I was too busy drinking in the countryside to indulge in talk. Smoke curled into the air, hanging motionless above the treetops, a blackbird warbled from the roof of the hut, from the nearby fields a curlew rose in a trembling ecstasy of song.

When we sang 'Taps' round the flag, the well-known words took on a new meaning for me in the tranquillity of that perfect evening. For the first time I had seen the sun slip quietly below the curve of the hills. With its going it seemed to take away my inner turmoil. How could I help but feel that all was well and that God was nigh in that peaceful meadow where the birds of the air and the animals of the field held precedence over all else?

My tent-mate was a round little girl called Janet. Her moon-like face creased into smiles at the pantomime I treated her to as I undressed. I was able to do this for myself now though less than a year before I'd had to rely on Mam to remove difficult things like jerseys, because it was beyond me to raise my arms above my head.

Now I could remove all my garments unaided, but the contortions I went through in the process might possibly have earned me a place in a circus. The struggle into the gay little gingham sleeping bags was even more of a challenge so Janet helped me twist into my bag then I leaned perilously far out of bed to help her into hers.

The majority of the Guiders were over at the hut because many of the girls had to be undressed and generally helped, but Miss Forsyth and Miss Graham appeared at the door of our tent. The former was a tall lithe bundle of energy nicknamed 'Snowy' because of her mop of silvery hair. She was a creature of gentle appearance with a pink and white complexion and a soft cultured voice. Her workmanlike camp overall and large wellington boots in no way robbed her of her ladylike appearance. By comparison Miss Graham had a lived-in face and a well-worn figure but she was the essence of good nature and her bright toothy grin was like a warm beam of sunshine. 'Anyone in here like a hot bottle?' she asked tucking away a strand of iron-grey hair. 'The water's on the boil.'

'Me, please,' I said promptly, because the lumps of flesh that were my feet were always cold. In minutes a hot bag appeared and I snuggled down blissfully. At my request, the Guiders left the tent flap open, and it was lovely to lie in comfort looking at the silhouette of trees against a sky that would never really grow dark that night. A flight of geese lazily winged their way past in perfect orderly formation, as harmonious as a team of stunt aeroplanes.

Never had I known anything so incredibly peaceful. Thoughts of Mam winged to mind but didn't disrupt my happy contentment. The memory of her gentle, undemanding love was a balm to my soul. My feelings of guilt for going off and leaving her had been of my own making for she certainly hadn't given me any reason for them. She had made it quite clear that she wanted only my happiness and, while my whole being demanded that she share the good things with me, my better sense told me that it couldn't always be so. I was growing up; inevitable my world would revolve round more than the family circle.

My thoughts were shattered by shrieks of laughter from the Guiders gathered round the fire near the edge of the field, Wullie's voice soaring out of the general hubbub. Janet and I shot up in bed to crane our necks curiously, but the twilight played tricks with the eyes, and it was difficult to make sense of the jumbled array of figures in the distance.

In the morning we learned that Wullie had tripped over a log while stepping backwards and had landed without the least intention in a pail of cold water. Her posterior, being somewhat broader than the rim of the pail, jammed tight, and her plight was so comical the others had been unable to go to her aid till they had recovered sufficiently from their laughter.

The breakfast scene was hilarious as the escapade unfolded in Mrs Winters's colourful language. 'I've made up a rhyme about it,' she concluded. 'Who would like to hear it?'

There was a roar of encouraging sounds and she proceeded to chant, 'Always look before you leap! Before stepping backwards . . . take a peep! If you don't your heart might fail . . . when you land in a cold cold pail!'

Everyone shrieked delightedly and a spluttering Wullie, her face cheerfully pink as always, said, 'I've got a better one . . . listen. "There's a thing you never ought'er, land yourself in a pail of water! If you're broad around the stern . . . you might never get out again!"'

'Great!' we applauded, and spent the remainder of the breakfast hour making up silly verses.

The days that followed were full of laughter and pleasant tasks. Each Patrol had a nature log to keep and we kept our eyes well open when we were taken for rambles in our chairs.

I was at the stage now where I resented being pushed along, contrarily only welcoming a helping hand when I came upon hills, pot holes and bumps. My chair was a new one issued by the Ministry of Health. It was small and easily manoeuvred and I wanted the world to see how well I could manage it. Although wheelchair-bound, I didn't feel disabled. I hated being fussed over and told I couldn't possibly do this or that. Fearlessly I sought to overcome all obstacles, using the most outlandish methods to further my ends. I loved to whizz down hills in glorious abandon. If my brakes didn't stop me then I used my feet. My Guiders paled incessantly but knowing my fierce independence they reprimanded me quietly but admirably refrained from ordering me outright to stop my antics. To put it simply, I was a non-conformist. I never would fit into the pattern of how a disabled person should think, act, look. If a place was inaccessible for a wheelchair, I would get down on my hands and knees and crawl to it. If my feet didn't stop me on my downhill excursions then I used my hands on the wooden rims of my wheels, sometimes to such a degree that my palms almost went on fire with friction. Hacks, blisters and corns scarred my knees and hands, but I had long ago ceased to fuss about such minor ailments. When the other Guides huddled in the marquee during rainy spells, I sat outside, lifting my face to the cool wet drops in ecstasy. Although the looks on the Guiders' faces suggested that they thought I was quite mad, they resigned themselves to the fact that at thirteen years old I was a rather eccentric individual and I was allowed to enjoy myself in my own way.

Every new dawn brought fresh excitement. There were expeditions into the local village and treasure trails in and out of the leafy woods that bordered the field. On an outing with the Rotary Club, I bought Mam a fine sparkling brooch for the lapel of her good coat and an ounce of tobacco for Da, though I knew he would grumble because it wasn't his favourite thick black.

Every evening we made huge fires and sat in the gloaming savouring wood-smoke tea and eating singed sausages. I had taken to the country as if I had been born to it. Somewhere inside myself I felt I had known it all in another time, so attuned was I to the sights and sounds. Mam had told me once that there was gypsy blood in us from her side of the family. Her olive skin, green eyes, and naturally waving hair suggested that this might be the case. I had inherited her hair and her colouring. I felt there might be some truth in what she said because all my life I had been aware of a restless spirit which had found an outlet in my ability to dream of fantastic other lands full of wide open spaces and magic happenings. There had been this other feeling too, a vague feeling of searching for something and never quite finding it. The moment I saw and smelled the country I knew that my search was over. In the soft sough of the wind I heard my own voice, my spirit soared on the wings of the wild geese, my soul belonged to the vast infinity of open spaces. Nature created no noise, only sounds that were beautiful, from the scurrying of small insects in the long meadow grasses to the haunting melody of the curlew's song. For the other Guides it was perhaps only just a week of fun in the country, to be enjoyed while it lasted. For me it would last forever. Sitting beside human companions, rubbing shoulders with them, I laughed and sang, but the rays of gold and silver in the evening sky made my heart almost burst with the beauty of it. Some of me stayed with those dear people round the camp-fires, but my bigger part merged and became one with the countryside, while sadness and happiness fought for supremacy in my soul.

Perhaps it was as well for me that I had been born with a strong sense of humour, or I think I might have been too solitary a waif. As it was, I found many things to laugh about. The other Guides looked to me for funny remarks and no matter how quiet I might feel inwardly, the extrovert in me had to comply.

But there were times I laughed my head off without the least intention. I was at the height of the giggly stage which was coinciding with the phase of hero-worship, a recipe which sometimes produced rather disquieting situations.

I was working for my Second Class badge at this time. Part of it entailed cooking a meal out-of-doors, the aim being to make it as succulent as possible with limited facilities and materials. Four of us set off to the woods, arriving at a little glade where the sun made patterns through the trees and a breeze scurried in gay abandon amongst the long grasses.

It was fun cooking the meal over an open fire, though the wood we had painstakingly gathered seemed to be making more smoke than flame. Nevertheless, after much fanning, we managed to produce a meal of sorts on the hottest stones. The big part of the test was still to come. Two of the Guiders had to sample the meal to find out if it was fit for human consumption.

I looked at the potatoes boiling in a billy can, noting with evil merriment that two flies had come to a sad end in the hot water. I fished them out with a spoon, relieved that I wasn't duty-bound to eat any of the food, though it was lunchtime and I was hungry.

Twigs snapped and two smiling Guiders came out from the trees. I was horrified to see that Mrs Winters was one of them. She was the latest victim for one of my schoolgirl crushes. Her presence filled me with awe. To me nothing was too good for her, and I was appalled at the thought of her tasting our singed potatoes and smoke-flavoured custard. The other Guides didn't seem to share my frame of mind and politely asked the two to sit down by the fire.

'Draw up a log,' grinned round-faced Janet engagingly, and the Guiders obediently sat down on a large tree stump. Plates were brought out and preparations made to serve the meal.

Embarrassment for myself in having had a hand in making the meal and affection for Mrs Winters rendered me speechless. I watched her prod her fork into a rather brown potato and a large bubble of mirth rose into my throat. Her strong teeth bit through the brown flesh and I heard a distinct crunching sound which told plainly that the potato was still raw in the middle.

The bubble erupted in my throat to emerge as a pig-like snort of pure helpless ecstasy.

'Are you all right, Chris?' asked Mrs Winters anxiously. I couldn't answer. Through blurred vision I saw that Miss Graham was having difficulty getting her ancient molars through the outer skin of her potato. My screech rang through the woods, bringing me both pain and utter unadulterated pleasure.

It was letting me down again, my blindingly vivid imagination that could conjure the most ridiculous pictures from words and gestures. It had been the cause of many a belting from little Miss Black in days gone by when my giggles distracted the class and I was sent marching to her room for my punishment, usually a 'doubler' which sent her long skirt billowing out like a tent.

Facial expressions also held an irresistible fascination for me and as these were usually associated with the human animal I was always bringing disgrace upon myself.

The sheer solemnity of this particular occasion only served to intensify my merriment, but gradually I sobered and felt shame reddening my face. I had made a fool of myself before Mrs Winters, but she and Miss Graham seemed unaware that I had just laughed myself into exhaustion. They were making suitable sounds of appreciation over the lumpy custard. Another bubble rose in my gullet, but I choked it to death. The meal was over and we would all have to wait for an official verdict before we knew the results of the test.

Mrs Winters seized my chair and began pushing me through the woods. She leaned over me and said with an adorable grin, 'Don't worry, Chris, old thing, when I was your age I caused my family great concern by having giggling fits at the most unsuitable times. Once I almost died laughing when my father nearly choked to death on a prune stone. My mother despaired of me ever growing to be a lady . . . and, as you can see, she was right.'

My face grew hot with pleasure at having been let into such a personal secret, my heart fluttered with love, and I let out inarticulate sounds of joy as we wended our way over the leaf-strewn path.

The day before camp broke up, wheelchair sports were held in the courtyard of the old stables. We began with an egg and spoon race, with the Guides holding the spoons in their mouths while the Guiders raced us along to the finishing post. As the chairs had a marked preference for going round in circles, this was not achieved without a good deal of hilarity.

After this the Guiders donned blindfolds and with them pushing us we had to direct them along. In the excitement many of us got confused with right and left instructions and we had a merry time colliding with each other.

When the junior races were finished we sat on benches and the Guiders got into our chairs for their own events. With more enthusiasm than expertise, they whizzed around in circles, bumped into each other, and generally had a lot of fun. They then finished off the morning with the three-legged race, tripped, fell, and staggered about, with Wullie and Snowy eventually rolling to the finishing line where they lay, unable to move for laughter.

Later in the day we had tea in the rose garden. It was a place of delicate colours, glorious scents, and utter peace. Bees trailed in and out of the fragrant blooms, their unhurried passage from flower to flower enhancing the sense of tranquillity.

We ate dainty sandwiches which I could have gobbled in one bite, but social etiquette was called for. I nibbled daintily, though when I saw Wullie take unashamedly big mouthfuls I giggled quietly. A week of fresh air had given us all healthy appetites.

Tiny cakes and pink ice-cream disappeared in no time. Then followed a tour round the gardens where rockeries were ablaze with colour and shrubberies sent generous whiffs of mock orange and lilac into the air.

Mrs Winters gave a vote of thanks to the lady and gentleman whose kindness had made possible that lovely week of camp.

The day was rounded off with a huge tangy camp-fire. Flames leapt into a sky of deep blue velvet. I listened to the crackling logs and my heart was as full as on my first day of camp. I wanted to see Mam again, to tell her of my wonderful experiences, but I knew my heart would pine for the country when I was back amidst the grey tenements of my childhood.

Oh God, I thought, please let me come back to the country one day. I belong here. I don't want to be self-ish but I wish I had been born where the sky is everywhere . . . not just above the chimneys.

A song broke into my thoughts, soaring sweetly into the dreaming night. Tears of gratitude filled my eyes because although the tune was familiar the words were different, written by me during a rest hour. Mrs Win-ters looked over and winked, Snowy's head gleamed silver in the firelight, Wullie's pink face was thrown back in a moment of solemnity, and all I wanted to do was bury my face in my hands and cry. But I sang instead, feeling close to the dear people who had given so unstintingly of their time so that children like me could know the joys of the countryside. The song ended and everyone looked at each other in a moment of sadness. The last night, the last camp-fire.

'C'mon everyone,' said Mrs Winters cheerily. 'Three cheers for such a jolly week and three cheers for our next camp!'

Everyone complied loudly but inwardly I thought, The next camp! A year away! How will I *live* till then?

A Small Hope

Two years passed, years full of Guiding activities, summer camps, and many hours of boredom in between. I thought less and less of past days when I could run like a hare. I was referred to as a 'cripple'. Oh, ugly word! It belongs to the Middle Ages and should be struck out of the modern-day language altogether. But I had resigned myself to life in a wheelchair and my feelings were somewhat mixed when my doctors wanted me to go into hospital for an operation to try and straighten one of my legs. If it was a success, another would follow on the other leg. All along a small hope must have lurked that one day I would get back on my feet, but I didn't want anything to do with hospital while my life was reasonably full. 'One of these days,' I told myself, and immediately put the thought away again.

Now the time had come, a decision had to be made. I wasn't afraid of the operation, though the doctors warned Mam it would be a big one, the major surgery I had thought sounded grand in a silly childhood fancy. Mam, always the soul of diplomacy, told me the final word lay with me, but in the next breath said, 'You're growing into a bonny lass, Chris, just think of all the loons waiting to dance with you.'

Kirsty came bursting into the kitchen just then, green eyes sparkling, cheeks pink from the walk home. She had been out dancing, and whirling my chair round in a moment of abandon she told us she had met a 'smashing boy' and was going out with him the following night. My mind had been made up before her appearance, but listening to her I became more determined than ever to go through with the operation. Now it wasn't the thought of needles and enemas that frightened me. It was the idea of meeting a lot of new people. Though the Guides had given me back my self-confidence, I was still painfully shy with strangers. I was impulsive in many things but never found it easy to make friends and was always scrutinizing my appearance to reassure myself.

Kirsty danced into the scullery to make the bedtime cocoa and I grabbed a mirror to stare at myself. Da was always telling me I was getting 'big-heided', but I paid no heed to him because I knew I was growing quite attractive, my best features being my grey-green eyes, smooth tanned skin, and my long waving hair which received so much brushing Da warned me, 'Ye'll pull the bloody lot oot by the roots.' Now almost fifteen, I was still very thin, childishly so for my age. I had no bust though I longed for one, regularly looking to see if by good luck my 'pimples' were growing into little hills.

My brothers teased me in the horrible way that brothers have. 'Found any bosoms yet?' Ian asked constantly, to which I would ably reply, 'One day I will but you'll never get a new face. You ought to stop taking ugly pills.'

Both Alec and Ian had put Kirsty through hell while she had been in the process of developing, but it was easier for me being the second in line and I was able to give the boys smart replies. The doctors said I was a slow developer because of my illness but I would grow into a woman if all went well. There had been no sign in recent years of overactivity of calcium and the medics were confident that my disabling illness had now burned itself out.

The time soon came for me to go into hospital and I was admitted to a surgical ward that seemed to stretch into infinity. White beds marched on forever and my heart flipped over with apprehension. God! I thought, There's *millions* of people here!

'Welcome tae Argyle Street!' said a cheery voice, and I treated my immediate neighbour to a sickly grin. Her bed-clothes were humped over an enormous cage, open at the bottom to afford a perfect view of a plaster-encased leg, open a slit to let her wriggle her toes. Her face was very pale, the bright red lipstick and rouge making it mask-like. Black hair tumbled in a cascade over the white pillow, matching the thick dark mascara that clung to her lashes. She was possibly only in her late thirties but I was young enough to think that she was quite antiquated.

'They've got me trussed up like a bloody chicken,'

she said cheerily, indicating the cage and the saline drip attached to her arm. 'I only got my operation yesterday but I'm scunnered wi' bed already.' She leaned up on her elbow to look at me. 'You watch it in here, hen. They're a bunch o' hot totties for rules and regulations. When they were preparing me for my op one nurse said, "Ye'll need to take aff yer make up, Mattie. Ye canny go tae theatre like that." Know what I told her? I said, "Away tae hell! The Gods might see my bum but they sure as hell won't notice my face." Is that no' right, hen?' I giggled in agreement and she continued, 'What are ye in for? Is it yer legs? I saw ye being wheeled up on a chair.'

'I'm to have an operation to try and help me to walk again.'

'Aw! Can ye no' walk? That's a shame! Never mind, they'll no' be long in cuttin' ye up,' she grinned maliciously. 'They hack ye to bits, sew ye up and expect ye tae live! No fear o' peace either. It's worse than Sauchie on a Saturday night. Trolleys whizzin' aboot! Doctors pokin' yer belly! Nurses jaggin' ye on the bum every five minutes! As for privacy, they havny heard the word here. I'm glad I havny got wallies because they take them away to the lavvy to clean them. They could get mixed up and you'd be puttin' somebody else's wallies in yer heid! Do *you* call that hygienic?'

'Er . . . no,' I spluttered, storing up all her quaint chatter so that I could relate it to Mam.

She moved restlessly, chewing gum with a fervour

that matched her quick tongue. 'Is yer mammy comin' the night?' she raced on. 'My man goes tae the boozer first then shows up at the last minute and gies me all his worries. The weans are all at death's door accordin' tae him. I blame his cookin'. Tinned beans and greasy links! It's all he can make for the poor wee souls!'

She wiggled her toes energetically and said disgustedly, 'I wish I had a fag! One wee drag and I'd be happy. I asked that wee fat nurse tae put the screens round me so that I could have a puff but she wouldny hear o' it. Feart I'd set the bed on fire! Ye'd think ye were straight oot the loony bin . . . still,' she smiled, 'at least ye get yer grub served up . . . even though it's mair suited for the pigs!'

In the week that followed Mattie was a ray of sunshine in a world that was too busy or too ill to be bothered with small talk. The nurses were friendly and attentive but were forever being called away and the other patients, in various stages of recovery or apprehension, couldn't be bothered with fun.

The day of my operation came at last. I was anxious to have it over with but couldn't help the butterflies that churned in my belly when the nurse came to prepare me for theatre.

Mattie, up and hobbling about now, popped her head round the curtains, her ready smile tinged with sympathy. 'Is it no' awful the way they dress ye up, hen? Ye feel yer goin' oot for yer Hallowe'en. I felt a right mug wi' my goonie and fitba' socks . . . how are ye feelin'?'

'A bit . . . funny,' I gulped as the nurse added the finishing touch to my theatre garb, a large white cap into which she tucked all my hair. She smiled. 'There, now you're all set.' She turned away. 'I'll be back in a minute to give you an injection that will make you feel nice and relaxed.'

'Mair like flaming drunk,' said Mattie sympathetically. 'But I must admit it's a nice feelin'. Just kid on ye're going to a party tae get sloshed!' she chuckled. 'Is it no' terrible the way they shave yer bum? Mine are just startin' tae grow and it's awful itchy. My man says it'll be like makin' love tae a clothes brush!' She laughed again and scratched immodestly. 'Keep yer pecker up, hen,' she instructed cheerily. 'See ye soon.'

The nurse came back with a syringe, the needle pierced my flesh and before long I was floating on a hazy cloud, my last minute fears fading into insignificance.

Vaguely I knew the trolley had come to take me to theatre. Masked figures made appropriate jokes but I was too drugged to do more than mumble drunkenly. Swing doors opened to admit me into a brightly lit room. I got a vague impression of a huge circular light dominating a white ceiling. I knew I was 'there' and in a mild panic raised my head to stare at rows of gleaming instruments. In a dream I saw gowned and masked figures floating about. One came towards me, an anonymous head blotted out the light and a detached but kindly voice said, 'Time for arithmetic, Christine. Can you count to ten for me?' I knew he was about to give me the anaesthetic and I welcomed the deliverance it would give me from this strange world of floating lights and ghostly people.

'In a few minutes,' I told myself, 'they'll be cutting me up, my blood will be everywhere but I don't care because I won't be here to see it.' I smiled at my own weird logic then began to count, 'one, two . . . three . . .' The anaesthetic swept over me, engulfing my senses and real fear choked me. I struggled to shout out, the anaesthetist's voice soothed me, then I moved into a world of oblivion.

Struggling through the remnants of the anaesthetic I awoke while I was being wheeled along a corridor. Surprised, I saw a nurse walking alongside holding aloft a bottle of plasma. It was only when I was being lifted into bed that I realised the blood was dripping into me.

I was in a little side ward containing three other beds besides mine. The curtains were whipped round me, doctors fussed with needles and drips and slowly I sank into the abyss of sleep once more. Sometime during the night I wakened to see a doctor sitting at my bed with my wrist between his fingers. I looked at him through half-shut eyes, noting his dark curly hair and brown eyes. The night sounds of the hospital came to me, the banging of a distant door, the muted clatter of cups, footsteps along the corridor, a soft groan from somewhere near at hand. Suddenly I felt wonderful. I was alive. Eyes and ears proved it. I became aware of clinical smells, the most prevalent being the faint smell of anaesthetic that lingered round me. The fear I had before the operation, that of not wakening from the anaesthetic, now seemed ridiculous, and my heart sang with joy.

'How are you feeling, Christine?' said a voice at my side, a quiet, cultured voice that blended with the solitude of the night.

'Great,' I assured the cool, white-coated figure who owned the voice. 'How long was I in theatre?'

'About five hours, it was a long job. Do you have any pain?'

'No . . . none,' I said, surprised. Gleefully I told myself if this was all there was to a major operation, then I would gladly go through one again. I concentrated my thoughts on the newly operated leg. I knew it was in plaster because I could feel the cloying folds of it against my flesh, but otherwise the limb was void of sensation. For what seemed like hours I chatted to the doctor, my tongue looser than that of a drunk. He told me that Mam and Mary had been phoning, also some of my Guiders. 'You're very popular, Christine,' he said with an engaging grin and lying there, in the clinical hospital bed, my leg encased in plaster, tubes dripping blood and saline into me, I thought he was the handsomest young doctor I had ever seen.

Very soon, however, I ceased to have any feelings for anyone but myself. Pain burned in great throbbing waves through my leg. I knew the doctor was watching me and something told me he had been waiting for the symptoms I was now experiencing.

My world became full of pain that grew in intensity till tears flowed from my eyes and I moaned in despair. I was given an injection of morphine; once again I floated and my senses slipped away. For days I lived in a drugged haze, longing only for the drugs that eased my pain and the blessed sleep that claimed me after each dose. Food wouldn't stay down. I was repulsed by the very smell of it. Glucose drinks were my mainstay.

My family came to me but it was beyond my capabilities to speak to them or acknowledge their presence. They spoke but their voices seemed to come from a long distance. Desperately I made supreme efforts to communicate but my voice came out in a croak. Mam's beloved face hovered and her hand smoothed the hair from my hot brow. 'Don't try to talk, Chris, my lamb,' she said quietly. 'We're all here. I won't go away from you. Try to sleep, you'll be better soon. It was a terribly big operation but,' she made an attempt to smile, 'it will be worth it. You'll give the loons a dance yet.'

'No, Mam,' I cried silently, 'don't raise your hopes too high.' It was some time before I wanted to come back to the land of the living but my need for the world was stronger than my pain and one morning I woke up and told a nurse I was hungry. Willingly she went to get me tea and toast and sat on my bed while I savoured every mouthful. 'I'll tell Mattie you're with us again,' she said happily. 'She's asked every day to see you, driving us all crazy with her questions.'

Mattie's intrusion into the little side ward was like a sudden gust of wind on a calm day. She battered through the door, the rubber pads of her crutches making squelching sounds on the polished floors.

'You no' up yet, ye lazy bugger?' she imparted delightedly, ignoring the look of horror from an elderly lady in the next bed. 'My God! Some folk are born wasters! First ye sleep like a log for days on end then ye lie aboot lookin' like ye'd never left yer bed since the day ye were born! Is yer leg any better?'

'It's stopped giving me so much hell,' I returned, feeling nicely wicked on uttering a word that was so utterly foreign in the deathly quiet of the little room.

'Aw, that's good,' said Mattie, throwing herself on to a chair and depositing her crutches against the neighbouring bed. The action earned another look of disapproval from the elderly lady and Mattie said loudly, 'We'll need tae get ye oot o' here, hen! It's like a morgue . . . no' the kind of place for a young lassie!' She lowered her voice to a diplomatic whisper. 'I'm right fed up in here, Chris. I was in the lavvy this mornin' when an auld wifie chapped the door and started shoutin' the odds. She had the skitters and was on at me to hurry for fear she would mess her breeks. *Two* other empty lavvies but the blind auld bat couldny see them for lookin'. Ye canny even get a *pee* in peace!'

Her voice had grown louder in her vigorous throat and as her words fell on the ears of my neighbour she humped her back and dug her nose into a book.

I giggled and gasped, 'Och Mattie, that wife won't look at me again but I don't care. You've given me the best laugh I've had in ages.'

'That's what I came for,' she intoned triumphantly. 'Nothing like a cackle tae make ye feel better. When ye're back in the big ward I'll gie ye some mair but ye'd better hurry for I'm goin' hame next week. I'm away for a puff now but I'll be in touch. Don't let the excitement in here go tae yer heid! I've seen stuffed dummies wi' mair life!' She stomped away, leaving my three ward-mates to look at each other meaningfully.

'It takes all kinds,' sniffed a lavender-haired old lady, and I earned further disapproval by muttering a heartfelt, 'Thank God.'

Next day my bed was taken into the big ward and placed next to Mattie's.

'Welcome hame, hen,' she smiled as she helped the nurse to arrange my locker. 'Take yer finger oot yer nose and have one o' my chocolates. A present from my man! I near died wi' shock when he gave me them.' Taking a chocolate from the proffered box, I felt good to be alive. Mattie's rough and tumble nature was just the tonic I needed. Her repertoire was a mixture of curses and moans but her eyes twinkled all the time and she was a great favourite with both staff and patients. Several days later my plaster was removed, the wound cleaned and dressed and a new plaster fitted. This was to keep my leg straightened. Pain had diminished till it was a bearable throb. Intermittent pains seared through my foot, which I thought was strange till I learned that several important nerves had been severed under my kneecap, resulting in a 'dropped' foot.

The wound in my leg stretched from under the kneecap to the base of my left buttock. When the stitches were removed it was discovered that the delicate tissues surrounding the hamstrings had failed to knit, resulting in a raw sore. Skin grafts were talked about but discarded because my general health was poor, which meant a lot of time might pass before the wound healed completely.

During this period Mattie went home, moaning and cursing to the last but tears in her eyes when she bade me farewell. 'I'll come and see ye, hen,' she told me with a watery sniff. 'And ye'd better be up on yer pins or I'll skelp yer wee bum. The Gods didny cut ye up for nothing, ye know! They like their pound o' flesh!' She laughed and went off. As good as her word, she breezed in to see me on several occasions, but each time I was unable to tell her I was 'up on my pins', for I had not been allowed to put any weight on my leg.

My days were spent with the limb in a sling, my plaster now sporting the autographs of staff, patients, and visitors.

At the end of five months the hard shell of plaster was removed and I was sent to physiotherapy for electric treatment on my dropped foot. It was an agonizing business, with each tiny electric shock piercing my numb muscles to bring the foot up with a jerk. I dreaded the treatment. Anyone who has experienced an electric shock will appreciate my meaning. Doctors congregated round my bed now, gently easing the limb to its fullest extent, but it was only fractionally straighter than before and I knew such a slight improvement would never enable me to get my foot flat on the ground.

Mam was told that the operation hadn't been a success. Until better methods were devised to straighten retracted limbs, my days would have to be spent in a wheelchair. Mam hadn't the heart to tell me. She looked sad during this time. Later I learned she blamed herself for having encouraged me to go through such major surgery. But I blamed no one. It had been a gamble, one I would have taken anyway. To walk again! It would have been wonderful, but things were to happen to me, lovely things that would never have been had I been an 'able bod' like everyone else.

One day, at the end of a six months' stay in hospital, the doctor whose handsome face had floated before me after my operation sat on the edge of my bed and gave me an apologetic grin. 'Christine,' he began hesitantly, 'we're going to let you home. Surgery hasn't done your leg much good, I'm afraid. You've been through a lot . . . no one could blame you if you feel disappointed . . .'

In a moment of hot, heart-fluttering confusion, I grabbed his hand and said, 'Don't worry about it, doctor. I know anyway. You've all done your best . . .' Briefly I marvelled at myself. Me! Christine Fraser! Talking to a God the way I would talk to an ordinary human. Slowly I went on, 'I did hope but I've done that ever since I was a wee girl. But there's no use fretting about it. I've become used to a wheelchair . . . I'm quite a lazy person really. It's quicker to whizz along in a chair, and just think of all the shoes I'll save.'

Relief relaxed his features. Perhaps he had expected a tearfully dramatic scene, the kind in ancient movies with injured heroines tearfully proclaiming that their place in life was finished. Once, at a very impressionable age, I had watched such a film, had cried my eyes out as I watched the frail young heroine falling about and being fussed over by family, lovers, friends. I had been thoroughly misled into thinking that true-life tragedies must be like that, but now I knew that reality was very different. I had learned very quickly that no one had time for self-pity. It was shunned like a contagious disease and a person who harboured such feelings could never possibly know happiness.

My real regret was the time wasted in hospital.

Another half-year of my life had gone with nothing to show for it but an extremely long scar and a 'funny foot' that hung down in pallid helplessness. It would be quite some time before it would be half as good as before.

Partings

It was in the early autumn of 1958, a week or two after I came out of hospital, that a God-sent opportunity took Mam and me on a never-to-be-forgotten holiday. It was to a home in Dunoon where disabled people could go for a break. Each of us was allowed to have a helper so Mam came with me. Her eyes sparkled in a way they hadn't done for many a day as she pushed me around the little coastal resort on the Clyde. The salt air brought a glow of pink to her cheeks. To have someone else cook and serve her meals filled her with child-like delight.

Da couldn't be on the holiday with us but one day he came on the boat with Margaret, she tall and awkward in adolescence, he old at eighty-one yet still tall and proud, his clothes neatly pressed, his watch chain sparkling brightly.

The four of us went into a tearoom, feeling very extravagant. Mam, Margaret and I made a quick though expensive decision but Da pondered long over the menu card, until in the end he ordered fish and chips to be rounded off with ice-cream. When the latter finally came he sucked at it happily, taking no notice when Mam kicked him under the table and hissed at him to be quieter.

'Ach, weesht, Evelyn,' he said placidly, 'I canny help it. My mooth wasny made for manners and I'm no' doin' anybody any harm.'

Margaret, in the throes of growing up, with every emotion extra-sensitive, reddened with humiliation when he let out a loud and satisfied burp, her expression showing that she felt herself responsible for every homely mannerism he displayed in public. He was wonderful for his age, yet we didn't realize it. Having grown up with an elderly father we couldn't see that the proud way he carried his years was something to be regarded as precious, a banner of independent strength that we had inherited.

When we left the tearoom he grabbed my chair, steering me in the direction of Dunoon's high street. Mam browsed happily over the attractive displays in jewellers' windows, content to windowshop because she never had the money to indulge in frivolities, though she loved jewellery and was never without it when she was out.

'Wait here,' Da directed outside one shop. When he came back he handed her a small package. It was a book-shaped brooch which opened out to show views of Argyll. It was inexpensive but she loved it. Her enthusiasm over the simplest gesture was touching. To give Mam a gift was full of personal reward because she made you feel so enriched by her gratitude.

We spent a pleasant day and it was plain to see that Da was loath for it to end. 'The hoose is funny withoot ye, Evelyn,' he told Mam. 'I canny sleep at night.'

She took his big hand briefly. 'Och, it's only for a wee while. I'm enjoying myself so much, John.'

'Ay,' he said awkwardly, 'ye deserve it.'

They caught the last boat home, both of them leaning over the rails while the seagulls wheeled and screamed around them. Da looked lonely though Margaret stood tall and strong by his side. She looked like his grand-daughter, too young to have much in common with him. I realized that the reason he missed Mam so much was because she was probably the only one who understood him completely. Without her, there wouldn't be much companionship to be had at home.

Mam shaded her eyes against the bright gleam of the sea. 'I wish Pop could have a holiday too . . . but I'm glad I'm no' going back with them. It's grand to know we have another week here. We must make the most of it, Chris.'

Our holiday coincided with the Cowal Highland gathering and we managed to get into the stadium to watch the events. The air reeled with the skirl of the bagpipes and Mam shivered. 'My, this brings back memories. When I was a lass it was quite common to hear a piper playing in the open air . . . that was a long time ago and I was beginning to think I'd never smell the heather again . . . after twenty-five years it's difficult to imagine what it's like. I'd love to see Aberdeen again but it's that bonny here it's made up for everything.'

I looked at her happy profile, noting the dark fringe of lashes over her incredible green eyes, the fine sensitive mouth, always ready to smile no matter how troubled her inner thoughts, her smooth olive skin, and her cloud of white hair shining like a halo round her head.

A lump came to my throat at her words. Twenty-five years of drudgery without a holiday to break the monotony, yet she had seldom complained. I wondered how she could have borne such a lifetime of self-sacrifice. She was a symbol of patience, a gentle soul who asked little in return for her years of giving to others. Perhaps her reward was the knowledge that she had brought us all through the difficult childhood years despite phenomenal difficulties. She had struggled, fought, protected . . . and she had won in so many different ways.

Later in the week she counted the money in her purse and decided it would just stretch to a bus run. We decided on the scenic tour that wound round Loch Eck and 'Ower the hill to Ardentinny'.

The driver was one of those obliging souls that are known as gems. He whipped me up in his arms, sang 'Here comes the bride', and dumped me carelessly in a front seat.

'C'mon now, sweetheart,' he said to Mam. 'Sit behind me and you'll get a rare view of everything.'

The day was calm with mist hanging over the trees. We topped a rise and saw the looking-glass that was the Holy Loch with Kilmun Hill reflected in a patchwork of colour. The road to Loch Eck was a dream of misty blue mountains and thick lush forestry. Purple heather grew in abundance everywhere, fragrant masses that were irresistible to golden-brown honey bees.

Loch Eck came to us suddenly, breaking through the trees, the dark green depths denying the reflection of the blue sky, snatching its unique colouring from the ochre-brown mountain furred with dark ever-greens. The unflurried surface of the loch created a perfect mirror which gave the beholder a double bounty of unspoilt perfection that claimed a place in my heart forever.

'Isn't it lovely, Mam?' I said joyfully.

'I'll remember this day and this place for the rest of my life,' she said simply.

The bus cut off at this point and began the climb into the hills. When I looked back the view was like something from a lovely dream with Loch Eck far below, the mountains etched against the heavens, and a little white-washed inn uncurling a banner of smoke that hung in tatters against the hills.

We chugged ever upwards into the heart of the forest till we came to a hairpin bend. Loch Long shimmered in the distance, framed on either side by heather mountains with endless rows of spruce marching ever upward. Then we came into a glen of clean tumbling rivers and tiny whitewashed cottages. Hairy brown cows browsed in the meadows. An eagle soared, a speck in the vastness of space but interesting enough to make the driver stop the bus so that everyone could focus binoculars.

Ardentinny nestled in a bay where the sea lapped to a shore of white pebbles. Brown children paddled in the wavelets, their cries of rude pleasure insulting the incredible peace of the place. Drifting gulls squabbled gently, tangy woodsmoke hung suspended in the still air, mingling agreeably with the piquant scent of pine-woods.

'If paradise is anything like this then I wouldn't mind going,' said Mam softly, her gaze taking in every detail on the journey.

All too soon the holiday was over, the sights and sounds of Argyll only precious memories. In the months that followed I had good reason to keep Mam constantly reminded of the good times that had been hers for a little while. It had been her first holiday in twenty-five years and the cruel twists of fate had already marked it down as her last.

Her illness came to her gradually but its progress would not be stemmed. It was the start of two torturous years for her and two years of unrest for those who loved her most. When we realized that it was not something that would get better with the passing of time, our lives became fraught with anxiety for this gentle soul who was the pivot round which our lives revolved. Like mine, her illness was rare, especially in a woman of her age. It was usually related to old age and Mam at barely fifty-two was still in the prime of her life.

The day she left to go into hospital my heart twisted with pain as I sat at the top of the stairs watching her being helped down by an ambulance attendant. She was very ill but her compassion for others was so strong she found the strength to help a small boy who had tripped on the stairs. Patting his head she said in her lilting voice, 'There you are, lamb, you're all right now.'

'Oh Mam!' my whole being cried out to her. 'I love you and you're going away and somehow I know things will never be the same again.'

Our house was strange and lonely without the presence of the one who made our poor little abode a home. The clock on the mantelpiece ticked with a frightening intensity in the silent kitchen. Her lovely crocheted bedspreads were no longer like gay flags but rather a too constant reminder of the patient hands that had fashioned odd bits of wool into things of beauty.

The smoke from Da's pipe hung like a black pall over the room, as dark as the clouds that had gathered in our hearts. His head was bent, his shoulders stooped, and he found a release for his tensions in irritable words that stung us to feel unreasoning bitterness. We were all on edge, ready to take umbrage at the least thing so that our emotions could be released in words of anger, anything to hide the awful fears that raged within us.

It was difficult for me to travel to the hospital but desperation goaded me into devising some method that would enable me to see Mam. Margaret, always willing to face a challenge, took me to the nearest bus stop where I hoisted myself on to a bus with the aid of the platform pole and swung myself round it like a monkey, so gaining the seat just inside the door. Margaret then folded up my chair and placed it in the little recess under the stairs. We became adept at this method for travelling on public transport and the bus seldom had more than the normal wait at the stop.

Each Sunday I went to the hospital and though Mam chatted cheerfully I knew she was failing before my eyes. She had undergone rigorous and extremely painful tests and though she was receiving treatment her illness was to get much worse before there was any sign of improvement. Her spirit was wonderful, her faith in God unbroken.

'I'll be better in a wee while,' she assured us frequently. 'Don't worry, I'll be home soon.'

Her locker bore an abundance of cards of one sort and another. On Mother's Day the whole family was gathered round her bed. Mary was a regular visitor and on that Sunday brought a huge bunch of daffodils with orange trumpets. Mam held them against her face, tears of gratitude in her eyes. She never ceased to be grateful that she was held in such high regard by her family. Ian took a picture of her holding the flowers. Later, looking at the resulting photo, we saw that her mouth smiled but her eyes were weary. Yet it is the expression in Mam's eyes that I remember most. They had always twinkled youthfully, even when encroaching years turned her hair to silver. Now, at the very depths of her illness, they shone with a deeper glow. It was as if her soul was using the medium of her eyes to prove that even though her spirit of endurance was undergoing its greatest test, she was winning through despite phenomenal difficulties.

But there were times when even her brave heart failed her and she sank into the crevasses of despair. One day she remained cheerful all through visiting, but when the time drew near for us to leave, tears sprang to her eyes and the words she spoke made my whole being cry out in fear. 'I don't mind dying now,' she whispered, holding on to our hands tightly in a plea for understanding. 'It would be lovely to be released from all this. I'd like fine to see my own mother again. It's been so long . . .'

'Don't talk like that, Mam,' I begged. 'You're going to get better.'

'No, Chris, my lamb, not in this world.'

We had to leave her like that, sad, lonely. When we turned at the door to wave she barely raised her head to look at us, her hand falling listlessly back to her side.

Da was a poor unhappy soul. He spent hours moping at the fire, his pipe hanging dejectedly from his mouth. The only time he brightened was when he prepared himself for visiting Mam. He began to look his age, his sprightly youthful appearance falling from him like a mantle. Now we saw how much Mam meant to him. His years of bullying reign over the household had become dim in our minds with the passing of time. His harsh words were now like the senseless marks on blotting paper and because we were growing up we were able to be tolerant about many things and saw that his blundering ways covered an inability to show his deeper feelings. In many ways he had shown kindness and consideration to Mam; now illness separated them and he was a lost lonely man.

He did all in his power for her, going out of his way to get the things she requested. She loved flowers, particularly anemones, and he took them to her, looking out of character with the tiny posies clutched in his big calloused fists. She called them 'annie-moonies', and gazed at the rich jewel colours with affection before placing the blooms tenderly in water.

While she was in hospital we heard that our name had come up on the Corporation housing list. It meant the chance of a bigger house with an inside toilet. The Govan house had become very unsuitable for me now because Da was no longer able to carry me up and down stairs. With the aid of a crutch I dragged myself up and down somehow, but it was a great effort and I was often a prisoner indoors, so I welcomed the news with delight.

'It will be great for Mam, too,' said Kirsty. 'We'll have a back and front door and a garden. You'll be able to grow flowers, Da. You won't need a window box any more. You can grow masses of Tom Thumbs and marigolds.'

We all felt better. Mam received the news with joy and immediately began to make plans for coming home. She was on a new drug that was proving very successful and when we saw how well she looked our hopes were high for the future. Her doctors were pleased at the news of the house, but told her to wait till the move was completed before even thinking of getting home.

We sifted through the collection of a lifetime, old things that we didn't want to take to our new home. Da refused to part with his pop-eyed, frightening pictures but Kirsty, now with a lash to her own tongue and an ability to speak her mind, told him in no mean terms that he could take the pictures but they were to be hung in his own bedroom.

'Less o' yer vinegar, ye cheeky bugger,' he told her with a return to his old asperity, but he said no more and Kirsty knew she had won the argument.

'Imagine having a house with five rooms in it,' I breathed in wonder, 'and a bathroom with a bath . . .'

'And a kitchen you'll be able to get into to help with the work,' said Kirsty with sarcasm.

'I can't help it if I can't get into the scullery!' I flashed back. 'Anyway, I do help with the work. I always do the spuds in a basin on my knee and you always pass out the dishes for me to dry! In fact I'm treated like a skivvy in this house . . .'

'That's enough, you two!' yelled Da, with a glare from his one eye. 'Get oot the trunk till I start packing. Fetch me some papers tae wrap my picters up in, I don't want them damaged. Alec, take these letters doon tae the midden and put a match tae them. I don't want any o' these nosy neighbours findin' oot my business. There's quite a stack so make a good bonfire.'

Under Da's growled instructions we gradually got things in order. Alec made several trips to the midden with old family documents torn into a thousand pieces, just in case anything escaped the flames so that the neighbours could swoop on the family 'secrets'. The Toilet Paper Lady watched our activities with interest, though she didn't look as glad as I thought she might be at our going. Perhaps the years had dulled her memories of my pranks, because she actually said to Da she was sorry we were going and he was to remember her to Mam.

Puffer watched all the proceedings with wary green eyes and I tickled her chin reassuringly and spoke affectionately to the little cat who had been my faithful companion for more than six years.

A week before the move to the new house Puffer became increasingly restless, padding from kitchen to room with a frown on her pussy face. She was sensing that a change was imminent and couldn't settle because of it. All her days she had been very much a home cat, only going out to relieve herself or to lie stretched on the sun-warmed dykes. During that last week she hardly left the house, as if afraid we would be gone before she returned, and her trips downstairs were only made out of sheer necessity. One afternoon she failed to return. Her fish was in her plate and normally the very smell of it was enough to bring her running. Margaret went out to call her from the landing. Her voice grew fainter and I knew she had gone downstairs. Minutes later she reappeared. She was crying, great tears running down her face and on to the limp little body of Puffer who lay still in her arms.

'What's wrong, Margaret?' I asked, but I knew the question was superfluous, a gamble for time to prepare myself for the truth.

'She's dead,' said Margaret tonelessly. 'For the first time in her life she crossed the road and a car must have hit her. She managed to make it back to the close . . . and just died.'

The last whisper of a breath dilated Puffer's dainty pink nostrils. For a moment we hoped for the hopeless, but she was gone. Gently I took the furry bundle into my arms and buried my face in the soft white fur of her belly. Pictures flashed through my mind: being wakened in the morning by a tentative paw patting my face; a warm purring scarf draped round my neck; a snoring bundle at the small of my back as I went about in my chair; a rough tongue washing my hands with brisk affection; everything gone in one careless moment of a little cat's life.

Quietly and sadly we placed her in a shoe box and buried her in a little plot of land nearby. In the days that followed we mourned for her. Even Da looked uncomfortably deflated when he found a ball of silver paper in the dross bucket. Playing with these balls had been one of Puffer's favourite games and to make sure she would never be without one she often hid a spare in the dross bucket. For a long moment Da stared at the little ball, perhaps seeing in his mind's eye a purring bundle twisting into the air to catch a silver ball tied to a piece of thread. Perhaps he was remembering times of loneliness when the warm heaviness of Puffer on his knee had brought a measure of comfort to an old man's life. Whatever his thoughts, they were deep enough to bring a large drip to his nose. He wiped it away with an impatient hand, then hurled the silver ball into the fire. 'There'll be no more damned cats,' he mumbled gruffly.

'No, Da,' I said sadly. 'There will never be another Puffer.'

He looked at me, surprised by my lack of argument, but I think he knew we were all too weary to have the strength for squabbling.

We were glad when the day came for us to move. With hardly a backward glance, we left behind the home of our childhood. I was lifted in my chair into the removal van beside what few possessions we had, and though I breathed a sigh of relief when I took a last long look at the tall grey tenements, I also felt a pang of emotion, knowing that the friends and neighbours we were leaving behind were people with warm hearts, always willing to lend a helping hand in times of need. I stared at our room window, feeling oddly sad to know that before very long another family would live in our house. Fleetingly I remembered the days of dummy parcels thrown from the window; of Mam's face hovering as she waved us on our way to the park; of Da's iron-grey head poking out in a search for his brood – and I wondered if his voice would find an echo over years of still, summer nights, when children played, heedless of time, unwilling to answer to the conventional demands of the grown-up world.

Jockey, our budgie, chirped loudly at my side, bringing me back to my present world. The van doors closed, shutting out the streets and the familiar buildings.

The new house was a five-roomed apartment with a long front garden, as yet desolate and bare. In a few weeks we changed all that. Kirsty became a keen gardener and bought plants and shrubs with enthusiastic extravagance.

'We'll need tae get marigolds,' said Da, as he pottered about getting in Kirsty's way.

'Ay, Da,' she said patiently. 'We'll get everything, but it will take time.'

When Mam was finally allowed out of hospital she

was greeted with a garden ablaze with colour. Pansies winked velvet eyes in welcome, the scent of roses dominated the air, and large orange marigolds splashed in vivid luxuriance against bright green foliage.

She stepped out of the taxi and came slowly up the path with tears of joy in her eyes. 'My, it's grand to be home,' she said happily, and the minute she stepped over the threshold our house was a home again.

She had a few weeks of happiness. All the things we never managed to have in our old home were hers to enjoy for a while. Kirsty had bought carpets and bits of furniture. The old chairs from the kitchen had been discarded, and Mam was able to sit in the luxury of a cosy armchair at last. Da hadn't wanted to part with the old chairs and he put up quite a battle to keep them, but it was more in the form of a peacock displaying its feathers to prove its superiority over the female. Mam couldn't walk very far but sat in the garden enjoying the sunshine. Margaret took her for walks in my chair and in the evenings she played the old piano that Kirsty had bought for my last birthday. But soon she took more and more to her bed, and I think each of us knew in our heart there would never be a complete return to health for her.

She lay in the bedroom upstairs, divorced from the rest of the household in a way she would never have been in the Govan house. We heard her singing to while away the weary hours. We all went to sit with her at different times in the day. The new house had a few drawbacks for a disabled person, the main one being the number of stairs between the living areas and the bedrooms. But I had devised my own method to overcome this obstacle. Sitting on the bottom step I folded my chair, and going upstairs on my bottom I pulled the chair up after me. A good deal of expertise was involved in the procedure. Unless properly balanced the chair fell over and I had several minor mishaps before I perfected the whole affair. Descending was even more precarious because the chair was liable to bounce down faster than I could follow and it was an arm-aching business keeping it under control. But I was undaunted. Anything that gave me independence was an achievement. I christened my stair-conquering technique 'bumming it', which was appropriate if not exactly lady-like.

Mam and I talked for hours. When we ran out of conversation we sang together. Sometimes I played the piano so that she could listen, and I often caught my breath on a tear when I heard her singing to the music. She was a prisoner in her room, yet her buoyancy of spirit somehow kept her cheery. Pain was a constant companion again and there came a day when she could stand it no longer and asked the doctor to let her go back into hospital.

She spent the entire winter there on various drugs. It was a dangerous merry-go-round. Too many drugs were needed to combat the symptoms of a disease that had started as a serious skin complaint but which had now spread inwards to bones and organs. At first the skin had peeled from her body, leaving raw flesh. Agonizing months of treatment had cleared her skin, but now that was the least of her problems. No one seemed to know exactly what had happened or what was going to happen next, and it was the not knowing that was the worst to bear.

Summer came round again, and I was due to go to the holiday home in Dunoon for a fortnight. I kept hoping that Mam would be well enough to come with me, and she didn't give up hope till the very last. Margaret took me to the hospital the day before I was due to go to Dunoon. Mam was in a little side ward and when we appeared her smile showed how pleased she was to see us. We weren't allowed to give her sweetmeats because she was on a diet, but we had picked a huge bunch of pansies from the garden.

'My, but they're bonny,' she said, stroking the velvet petals with a touch so gentle she might have been caressing the skin of a new-born infant. 'I can smell the earth in them, and the sun.'

She was full of hope that night, telling us she felt so much better she knew she would soon be going home. She spoke with such faith I was convinced she was on the road to recovery. I looked at her dear face and my heart soared. I told myself that everything would soon be as it once was, with Mam sharing our lives again; we would go to bed at night and know she would be there in the morning, the way it had been all through childhood, feeling a security as in the nucleus of the womb but aware of it in a way that one can't possibly be while growing in the silent world that is ours before birth.

Before leaving I took her warm hand in mine and looked into eyes that held peace and infinite love. 'Next year, Mam,' I said softly. 'Next year we'll go to the hills when the heather is in bloom. Don't give up hope.'

Her gaze held mine and everything that was life reached out in an eternal moment that made us one, a fusion of souls whose earthly bodies were of the same flesh and blood. 'Look after yourself, Chris,' she murmured. 'I'm so proud of you, my lamb. You've conquered things that would have floored a lot of folk. I'll be thinking of you . . .' Her eyes became faraway and she continued almost to herself, 'If only I could have seen the Grampians once again. In the autumn they're really purple with heather. I used to walk there . . . a long time ago . . . when I was a wee girl . . . just walk, picking the heather . . .'

I gripped her hand tighter and choked out, 'I'll bring you back a big bunch, Mam . . . for luck . . .'

'I've had my luck, Chris,' she said quietly. 'All there was meant for me.'

She kissed us both goodbye and I have often wondered if she knew she would never see us again. She had never been one for such demonstrations of affection, her kind of love had never needed them.

At the door we looked back and blew her a kiss. She

smiled, a happy smile, her hand lifted in farewell, her silver hair shining like a halo under the bed light. It is this picture of her I will carry in my mind for as long as I live, because it was the last time I saw her alive.

And she died alone, this dear, gentle mother of mine, alone in a hospital ward. She went with a struggle, for although life held so little for her she hadn't wanted to leave it. At the last minute she fought to keep it, but her weary heart would not allow it.

The news came to me in a telegram when my holiday was two days old. It took a long time for the words to sink into my fiercely resisting mind. Then I knew . . . I knew, but it didn't make sense.

'I wasn't with her!' I upbraided myself. 'She died with none of us beside her, only strangers who didn't love her! Oh God . . . why?'

Hours passed, one upon the other, but to me they might have been days. Kind people came to me like shadows in a dream. Impressions of arrangements for my return home were hazy incidents in time. The journey on the boat to Gourock was a nightmare. The dull throb of engines, the sea swaying the decks, phantoms moving and daring to laugh. I felt like an onlooker watching something unpleasant, and glad it wasn't happening to me.

Kirsty and Margaret had come to the station to meet my train but somehow we missed each other and I was fortunate to find a kind taxi driver who helped me into his taxi and folded my chair up beside him.

My nightmare became a reality when I arrived at the house at the same time as the vehicle bringing Mam from the hospital. I stared in disbelief at the coffin being carried in, and the echo of her last words came to me: 'I know I'll be going home soon.' She had gone home, right enough, but to one far removed from the humble little abode that had been hers on earth.

I came face to face with my family, and their white, strained faces reflected all that I felt. We were numb with shock and could say very little to help each other.

Later, I went up to look at Mam in her last sleep. She was very peaceful-looking. It was hard to believe that she wouldn't open her eyes at any moment and recognize me with a slow dawning of her wonderful smile. Her face was calm, free from lines of suffering, and I knew it was selfish to want her back. She had wanted this release, but I wanted her to be alive so that I could know again the thousand and one little things that were so endearing in her. It was then I cried, my face buried in her soft white hair, my heart a heavy pebble in my breast. Afterwards, I took a little lock of her hair and placed it in a little casket she had given me. It was a beautiful box, made of an inexpensive metal with a picture of Jesus enclosed in a tiny glass dome on the lid. I had often admired it and recently she had said, 'Here, Chris, you keep this wee boxie, I know how much you like it.' The action was typical of her. She had never placed much store on material possessions and was forever giving her things to us.

The sun shone on the day of her funeral, the birds sang, children laughed, life went on as usual, but for us a light had gone from the world, never to return. During her short stay in the new house she had made many friends, and her coffin was covered with wreaths from the neighbours. On top of all the elaborate floral tributes we placed a bunch of jewel-bright 'anniemoonies' and a spray of pink carnations from the garden.

The minister who conducted the service was an Aberdonian. He and Mam had enjoyed many a chat together, reminiscing about places that were familiar to them. He recognized in her a courageous spirit, with her trust in and loyalty to God beautiful in their simplicity.

The service was conducted in the house, but the minister's voice couldn't shut out the sounds of the coffin lid being nailed down, the trestles scraping on the floor over our heads and, finally, the coffin being carried downstairs. Our hearts went with her to a place far beyond the grave where her soul had at last found the peace it deserved.

Many months went by before we could bring ourselves to look at her pitifully few personal possessions which we had hurriedly scooped from her hospital locker. We found a parcel Kirsty had sent. It contained a new purse but had never been opened because it had arrived at the hospital on the day of Mam's death. All the letters and cards we had sent her were tied in a neat bundle because these were the things that she could never bear to part with. The sum of her life was in that well-fingered pile, and in the methodical collection of safety pins, elastic bands and recipes we found in her worn old purse. Tucked away in a corner were some verses she had written about her precious holiday in Dunoon, and an unfinished letter to me, a letter that read: 'The days are long and dreich, Chris, and I'll be glad when it's over. I can't see as well as I did, my eyes are easily tired. I think I'm growing old before my time, lamb. Some days I feel good but today I feel the old man heavy on my chest . . .' Here the letter tailed off, and with heavy hearts we abruptly ceased to look into the past. One line in Mam's letter held the key to her two years of suffering. She had hit on the truth without being aware of it. All along the doctors had told us that Mam's illness was one related to age. For it to happen to someone as young as Mam was a rare occurrence. The post-mortem had revealed that all her internal organs had aged long before their time.

To put it plainly, she simply died of weariness.

Black Maria

My life held a lot of loneliness after Mam's death. Da and I spent a great part of each day together, but we had little to say. He couldn't communicate with me, tell me about his grief, and I could not tell him the things closest to my heart.

I had a good deal to do with the running of the house. Ian had married a year before Mam died, the rest of the family were out at work. I had the meals ready for them coming home, and I kept the house as clean as I could, though I was unable to get upstairs to attend to the bedrooms. These were cleaned by Kirsty and Margaret at weekends. The house had an empty echo about it during the daytime. There was a coldness that had never been in the Govan room and kitchen. Deep in my heart I didn't really like the open atmosphere of a house that forced us to spread out at night, taking away the unity and cosiness that our Govan home had provided. Every morning Da plodded upstairs to bring me a cup of tea, an indication that he thought it was high time I was up and attending to the housework. The situation was ludicrous. I feared and resented the burden of responsibility on my shoulders, but could do little except make the most of my abilities. I felt sorry for Da, knowing how much he missed Mam, but I was unable to comfort him. He took himself off on lonely walks, his head bent, hands deep in pockets, unseeing, uncaring. At times he took to his bed, sometimes for as long as a week, and this in itself was an indication of how empty he felt. He had always hated laziness in any form, believing that activity cured all ills.

He was alone and I was alone, but I also had the terrible symptom of boredom to contend with. This wasn't a new thing in my life by any means. A prisoner in the Govan house, I could have screamed with frustrated boredom. With the advent of the new house I was perhaps even more tied, simply because my brothers and sisters now had their own pursuits to follow. There was no time to spare for the placid occupation of taking their wheelchair-bound sister out for walks. I longed to be out working and I had reached an age when I needed something more than the stimulus of my Guide functions, though it was perhaps these that kept me sane.

But even after death Mam was working for me. One of the last things she did was to write to the Ministry of Health, requesting that I be given some sort of transport to make me mobile. After some initial tests I got word that I was to be given an invalid car, and I was beside myself with joy. After months of waiting my heart sank to my shoes when it finally came. I had visualized one of the little blue three-wheelers powered by petrol and looking like a ‘real’ car. The one that arrived at the gate was like a bath chair from a funny old movie. It was black with a large hood which boasted yellowing perspex windows. It was powered by batteries. Steering, acceleration and brakes were operated by various twists of a long rod-like structure.

My disappointment was intense, and I felt myself go hot and cold with humiliation when the quaint object was immediately surrounded by a crowd of curious children. I grew even hotter as I pictured myself driving the monstrosity.

‘I’m not going out in *that!*’ I said to Da as we both peered from the window to watch the machine being unloaded, the proceedings hampered by the children who had already loudly called it everything from a scooter to a stagecoach.

How differently I had planned the scene. A gleaming blue three-wheeler should have arrived at our gate while neighbours peeked in admiration from their windows, the children silent with awe and respectfully envious.

Da sniffed, but his eyes showed a spark of interest that had been missing for months. ‘I think they dug that yin oot the ark, Chris. It’s a real auld-timer.’

‘I won’t go out in it,’ I repeated stubbornly.

‘Ach, away and no’ be daft,’ he scolded. ‘It’ll take ye oot the hoose. What does it matter how it looks if it’ll take ye tae new places?’

His voice was gruff, but his words were kind. Full

of curiosity, he went down the path and gave the vehicle a good going over. When he came back he had christened it 'Black Maria'. It lay in the shed that had been erected at the side of the building, and for almost a week I fought feelings of anger, shame, disappointment. I had been given instructions on how to operate the controls, and assured my instructor with a false enthusiasm that everything was perfectly clear. He watched me get into the vehicle and drive round the block in it. I had felt a small thrill at the motion of wheels and found the machine easy to manoeuvre, but my humiliation raced to the fore again when people turned to watch my slow progress, their looks verifying the fact that Black Maria was ridiculously out of place in a world of modern transport.

The installation of a power point to feed the machine was my responsibility, but electricians were expensive to employ so Black Maria stayed in the shed. The batteries lost their power. I couldn't make up my mind whether it was worth all the bother, so I didn't press the matter too far.

One night Ian arrived unexpectedly, armed with rolls of flex and power fittings.

'What are *you* doing here?' I asked with mixed feelings.

'Da asked me to come and fix up a power lead to the shed,' he replied, already starting work.

At his words I felt an odd pang of affection for Da. He was old, lonely, seemingly uncaring, yet he was concerned enough for my welfare to ask a favour of Ian so that I wouldn't be tied to the house. Ian had taken training in electrical work and soon had a power cable fixed up.

Tentatively I began going out in Black Maria, Da taking my chair back to the house because there was no room for it in the narrow little machine. Da peeked from the windows as I drove slowly away and I was reminded of another time when a lone figure waved me goodbye, sad yet glad that I was broadening my horizons. I was unable to go too far because of the limited power available, but the rural areas round Carmunnock were within my bounds. Driving through country lanes, I gloried in the scents of green fields and wild flowers. My love of the country wasn't a restless one. I was quite content to sit for hours looking at the many changes that weather conditions could bring to one landscape. To reach out and touch a leaf . . . that was ecstasy. To hold my breath as I observed some tiny wild creature . . . that was awe at the wonder of creation.

At weekends a member of the family accompanied me. It was strictly against Ministry rules to carry a passenger, but the presence of a near one gave me confidence to face that awful curious world one had to traverse before reaching green terrain. There was barely enough room for me in the narrow black seat, but with the aid of a cushion my passengers sat side-saddle and made the journeys very merry affairs, especially Mary who was always game for anything. Kirsty, on the other hand, wouldn't sit beside me for anything, though she couldn't help laughing when she watched the rest of us screeching to a halt outside the gate. That of course is a gross exaggeration, because there was so little power in Black Maria you could have stopped it with your feet like a scooter.

Uphill journeys were a real slog and it was then I had a following of cheeky urchins running to keep up with me while they kept up a colourful flow of rude comments. Though I never became totally immune to such unwelcome attentions, I took to the road almost every day, weather permitting. A long black apron affair gave some protection against the rain but I didn't fancy looking even more ridiculous muffled to the nose in black waterproof, with my rickety old hood making Black Maria sway in the wind.

But funny old Black Maria's days were numbered. I became daring in it, flying down hills at a reckless speed, certainly beyond the limits of safety for such a wobbly concoction on wheels.

One day Margaret and I set off to Carmunnock, she alongside me on her bike. The road there was mainly uphill which meant my homeward downhill journey was inevitably faster. We had a good afternoon in the country with a picnic and a lot of laughs. With Margaret there was always something to laugh at, because her devil-may-care attitude to life was a good partner for my impulsive nature and love of fun.

'I'll race you home!' I yelled. She immediately took up the challenge and began to pedal furiously so that she was ahead of me before I had quite realized what I had let myself in for. Soon I caught up with her till we were abreast, but it was downhill now and soon she was well behind, unable to keep up with my wild pace. My long hair flew behind me, my face tingled with the excitement of the race, and I roared to the skies with joy. Then came a moment of carelessness, that split second in time when the reflexes don't obey the message from the brain quickly enough. Our corner loomed, I fumbled to operate the brake but accelerated instead. In a series of mind-tearing zig-zags I swerved across the road to smash into a stationary car. In a jumble of impressions the shiny black bodywork of the car sped closer to my face, I kissed the boot handle with quite unintentional passion, then I was rolling about on the road with as much abandon as a heartily kicked football. Margaret skidded up to me and a lady pounded the tar on the road in a rush to get to me. They both grabbed me under the oxters and pulled me to the safety of the pavement, where I sat trying to collect my wits.

'What happened?' asked Margaret, in the sort of choked voice that was bottling up nervous laughter.

'I forgot my brakes,' I said with an insane snigger. My head had stopped spinning sufficiently for me to be able to see that Black Maria had crumpled like a concertina, the hood swinging crazily to one side, the front wheel deflating slowly with a tired sort of hiccuping hiss.

'Oh hell!' I said in dismay. 'What am I going to tell the Ministry?'

'Your face is all bloody,' snorted Margaret with a total lack of sympathy, 'and you're going to have a beaut of a black eye.'

I sat on the verge feeling as if my face had been kicked for weeks. I also felt extremely silly. Our Samaritan lady asked anxiously. 'Have ye broken something, hen? Can ye no' stand up?'

'It's all right,' I assured her shakily. 'I can't walk anyway and I haven't been able to stand for years.'

'She needs her chair,' said Margaret. 'I'll run home and get it . . . you stay here,' she directed me with a wicked snigger.

'Don't worry,' I returned sourly. 'I won't get up and walk away.'

'I'll bring ye a wee chair to sit in the now,' said the Samaritan lady, and scampered into a nearby close, to reappear in minutes with a kitchen chair. She helped me climb on to it and I sat there, in the middle of a housing scheme, at the side of the road on a kitchen chair, trying to look as if I did that sort of thing every day of my life.

'Here, ye look a bit shaken,' said the Samaritan lady, 'I'll away and get ye a cup of tea.'

She disappeared just as Margaret hove into view with my wheelchair. I welcomed it like an old friend, feeling oddly secure with my wheels round about me once more. Margaret went to peer at the car which had saved me from an unknown fate in a soggy roadside ditch. 'There's not a scratch on it,' she reported. 'Your wee buggy's taken all the bashing.'

'Thank goodness,' I said gladly, not in the least sorry for Black Maria. My worry was the Ministry officials and what they would have to say about the affair.

The Samaritan lady tottered out of the close, balancing a tray containing a pot of tea and a plate piled with biscuits. Her other hand held another kitchen chair which she plonked down beside me. 'I'll have a cup wi' ye,' she said companionably, and the three of us sat and chatted in the friendly way that Glaswegians everywhere are famous for.

Reluctantly I had to come back to practicalities. I decided it was time I reported my mishap to the Ministry. In those days, the body of Government officials who handled the affairs of disabled people were beings that I regarded with even more awe than the Gods I had once thought ruled supreme in hospitals. The Ministry Gods were a different sort from the medical Gods. The latter had your life in their hands, the former their hands on your life. Great decisions about your future lay with them. A visit to their clinic was designed to make you feel like a member of the KGB who had just dropped in to spy out the latest developments on the two-stroke engine or to sniff out the secrets of the non-squeak artificial limb. They measured methodically everything that could be measured in human anatomy. I know of course that this procedure is necessary to fit different-sized people into buggies and wheelchairs, but I hated the cold, precise way in which the whole business was carried out. To this day I often wonder how I ever got away without getting my head measured. Nowadays things are different. Like the medical Gods, the Ministry Gods have become exceedingly human, kind and helpful people, but then . . . shivers at the very idea of going up before the 'Officials'.

I couldn't persuade Margaret into doing the unwholesome task of phoning for me so, quaking in my wheels, I approached a telephone kiosk. The world and its amenities are undoubtedly geared to meet the needs of the very able able-bodied. I don't think even the great Houdini could have figured out a way to get a wheelchair into a phone booth. The GPO provides an excellent service but gives little thought to wheelchair-bound humans when they design their tight little boxes, and I wonder if some muscle-bound, Samson-like being was the first to open the tightly sprung doors of such creations and pronounce them fit for general use.

It soon transpired that the great Houdini had nothing on the great Christina. After I had recovered from the blinding flash of inspiration which struck me I crawled into the booth, Margaret folded my chair, and I sat astride the chair arms which fortunately for me were padded so I didn't suffer too much as I wobbled about while I dialled the number. Miraculously, I managed to give the coldly anonymous official on the other end of the line a fairly garrulous account of my accident, despite the hideous squashed faces that Margaret was making against the glass panes outside.

The mangled remains of Black Maria were scraped off the road and carted away. I felt no pangs of remorse because I'd never had any real love for the weird-looking old buggy. Perhaps that is why I treated it to such wild and careless handling, but whatever my reasons I didn't reckon with the resourceful Ministry repair shops. I had thought Black Maria to be mouldering in the scrap heap, but two weeks after the mishap she was delivered back to me, all the creases straightened out and looking as good as she ever would.

Disappointment raged through me. I had thought myself rid of the quaint vehicle, had expected the Ministry to give me something more suited to the faster pace of modern traffic. A few weeks later I learned my case had been reviewed and I was requested to go back to the Appliance Centre for a further physical examination.

Impatiently I awaited the results of the visit. Officials everywhere are good at forcing you to learn the gentle art of patience, but I had practised so much of that in my time I felt I'd had enough. Eventually the letter came, and it contained the mind-boggling news that my application for a petrol-driven three-wheeler had been granted. How I got through the months of waiting for it to come, I'll never quite know. Before each morning post I teetered on the edge of a smouldering volcano of emotions. Each unfruitful visit made by the postie brought me near to tears of frustration.

Quite often no letters came to our house at all and I sat at the window, watching the postie whistling his way past our gate, my heart cold and heavy at the prospect of having to wait for another day, another post. If I saw the postie open our gate and approach the door, all the life forces inside me were held in suspense at the click of the letter box. But I was sufficiently dignified and in control of myself to allow the postie to go down the path and shut the gate before I almost broke the sound barrier on my way to the hall.

How many bills and circulars I gazed at with tears in my eyes I'll never know, but one day *it* came, in a buff envelope, and the formal words telling me that my buggy was on its way filled my heart with their beauty.

A few days later it arrived at our gate, blue and gleaming, an apparition of such complete and miraculous wonder that for a long time I could do nothing but just look at it from the window, unwilling to rob myself of those precious moments of just savouring a dream come true.

But practicalities had to come and I soon realized that the workings of the new machine were much more complicated than those of Black Maria. To the layman these little invalid cars might appear easy to control. A lot of people are under the impression that they are automatic and all one has to do is push a magic button and off they go. The reality is very different. A good deal of effort was required for the push-pull tiller-type steering. Fortunately this was a left-hand construction. I was unable to straighten my right arm to its full extent so a right-hand tiller wouldn't have suited my particular case though, if necessary, the Ministry repairers were experts at adapting a machine to the user's needs. Throttle, clutch and brakes were all integrated on the tiller and the gears were to the right of the single seat, set in a straight-through ratchet-style housing. The battery was to the right of the seat behind the gears, with visibly large blobs of grease covering the terminals. The clutch fluid was contained in a small chamber at the junction of the steering column, covered by a rubber cap which I was to discover wasn't efficient enough to contain the red fluid which could so effectively stain clothing. Little thought had been given to the personal comfort of the 'invalid'. The upright seatback would have been perfect for a cross-legged, meditating Buddha, but as few 'invalids', or any sort of human for that matter, sit cross-legged or meditate while driving, the uncontoured seat was entirely unsuitable. A thin layer of rubber covered the metal floor which was badly sealed. Inclement weather brought whistling draughts and a swimming floor. There were no heaters in the little cars. The early ones, such as had been delivered to me, also had perspex windows through which force nine gales whistled with cruel abandon.

The general public who think that the majority of disabled people are delicate souls who cannot possibly live without every comfort in the book have simply no idea of the endurance tests that the handicapped go through every day of their lives. Later on, Jim Clark, the famous Scottish racing driver, proved in his campaign for disabled drivers that the invalid car was unsafe, unreliable and uncomfortable, to put it mildly. So think again, able-bods. Strength comes with a handicap – it has to or none of 'us' would survive.

I visualized none of the above-mentioned when I took delivery of Bertha Buggy, my pet name for the snub-nosed three-wheeler. My family were as thrilled as I was with the little car, yet there was a restraint in their attitude. They had all grown so used to me being around the house, a piece of the furniture, house-bound little Christine with the happy smile and the breaking heart I never showed . . . now I was about to spread my wings . . . things were going to change. Sometimes people, even one's own dear family, don't like change in the familiar run of things.

Da didn't say much at first but later on went out to examine Bertha thoroughly. 'That's a rare wee bus,' he stated grudgingly. 'The weans will no' be able tae run after ye in that.'

'It's a pity it's only got one seat,' said Mary on one of her Saturday visits.

At her words I looked balefully at the little notice on the dashboard which stated that passenger-carrying was strictly forbidden. The same rule had applied to Black Maria but I had broken it because it hadn't mattered so much. Bertha was different. I didn't want to do anything to risk the ire of the Ministry if I was spotted by an official carrying a passenger.

Ironically, there was just enough space to the left of the seat in which to place cushions or a small box, but I didn't want the awful experience of being on the mat for breaking the rules.

For a few joyful weeks I flew up and down country roads, revelling in the freedom that Bertha gave me, but the idea of getting a job was uppermost in my mind. Then I could be entirely independent. To date, I'd had to curb my fast-growing notions for fashionable clothing. My disablement allowance was almost totally absorbed into household expenses, leaving me little for personal spending.

Once more the Guide Movement came to my aid, my Ranger Captain arranging an interview for me in a small clothing factory at Hillington Industrial Estate. It was an establishment subsidized by the Government to train the disabled. I was accepted as a trainee overlocker, and quaking with nerves I went one morning to start my first day at work. I had never particularly wanted to be a machinist, but then I had never given much thought to what I wanted to do with my life. All my notions had been hazy and idealistic until the stark reality of growing up with no financial means had driven the dreams from my head.

I soon learned that I had been lucky to get training for a particular type of job. So often it was assumed that a dulling of the wits went hand in hand with physical disability. Some of the concepts that 'normal' people harbour about the disabled belong to the dark ages. Many employers came into this category. Wheelchairs, crutches and walking sticks are often regarded with reserved suspicion, though in most cases these accessories are only there to support actual human beings with properly functioning brains.

I liked my job, but I knew I would never love it. Often I was bored by the utter monotony of piecing garments together all day. It was too repetitive for my imaginative mind; for me I knew there had to be something else, but just then I was reasonably content. I was earning my independence and that meant a great deal to me.

Factory life was good for me in another respect. I was continually mixing with other people, able-bods as well as disabled. Double talk and backchat abounded. Shyly I groped for words but lacked the swift repartee of the others. I blushed easily, which brought inevitable teasing, and with my habit of listening rather than talking I soon earned myself the label, 'a deep one'.

My workmates were able to argue with the reassurance of believing themselves right. Confidence oozed from them and they enjoyed poking fun, usually at somebody else's expense. I listened and knew I would never be totally gregarious.

One day Lizzie, an able-bod who worked the pressing machine, pounced on my sleeping defences. 'You'll be the worst wi' the men,' she told me with a sort of mocking kindness. 'The quiet ones are aye the same. Look at ye, these big green eyes, that hair! I bet ye're a Jezebel!'

Rather naive for my eighteen years, I wasn't quite sure if it was a compliment or an insult, but I knew it had something to do with being attractive to men. Already I was receiving some admiring glances from the males in the factory and had experienced the first stirrings of my feminine powers, but Lizzie's words made me feel that I had been running around starkers, seducing all the men in sight.

'Ach, leave the lassie be.' Mary, the woman who was training me, rushed to my aid as I blushed crimson to the roots of my hair.

'It wis a compliment,' answered Lizzie in surprise. 'I wish somebody would think I was a vamp!'

Gradually, painstakingly, my shell of shyness cracked till one day I was able to give a swift retort to a derisive remark. My unexpected words earned a look of pained surprise from my tormentor, and she gave me the cold shoulder for the rest of the day, but from that point I had broken through the barriers. My natural reserve saw to it that I never really became 'one of the gang', but at least I was no longer the raw recruit I had been.

For long my mind had brimmed with all the wonderful things that would befall me if only I had transport. Now I had Bertha, but soon realized that the world wasn't going to come to me. I would have to meet it, but didn't quite know how to go about it.

My sisters went dancing every weekend. Arm in arm they went off, unintentionally shutting me out of their world. Each time I watched them go I felt a pang of emptiness at the prospect of another Saturday night indoors with Da.

Once Margaret persuaded me to go 'up the town' with her to a favourite dance hall. 'You can spectate,' she told me earnestly.

Off we went, she crushed in beside me on a box-cum-stool between my seat and the door. My need for company made me throw caution to the winds, though the 'no passenger' sign seemed to leer at me.

When we arrived at the brightly lit hall my courage almost deserted me, but Margaret was determined to get me inside. The doorman gave me a queer look and I smiled to myself. A wheelchair going into a dance hall obviously wasn't one of his everyday experiences. He proved to be very obliging, carrying me upstairs and depositing me on a seat inside. My chair was whisked away to a cloakroom, and I was left feeling very lost without my wheels around me.

The atmosphere was gay, full of whirling feet. The

music was loud but acceptable to young ears, and I felt a small thrill of excitement. Margaret was pounced on immediately by an eager young man. She was very pretty with her fair hair and shapely limbs. She was whisked away and I was left with the rest of the wall-flowers, but knew I looked more like a wild rose. I didn't look disabled. My legs were a little thin but there were no other signs to prove my disability. My hair was long, falling down my back in natural waves, my eyes an unusual grey-green, vividly alive in my tanned face. With no one of the opposite sex to reassure me about my looks, I constantly reassured myself by spending a good deal of time in front of the mirror. My figure had improved with the years, and I no longer needed to stuff cotton wool into my bra to improve my shape. Taking all this into account, I wasn't too surprised at being asked to dance several times in the course of the evening. One young male was particularly insistent and at one point grabbed me by the hands to pull me up before I knew where I was. But my arms were strong and we had quite a tug of war. My imagination began racing and I saw myself being whirled round the hall without my feet touching the floor, quite literally 'dancing on air'.

The picture made me snort with laughter.

'Whit's funny?' sniffed the youth.

'Nothing . . . just . . . I don't dance . . . honestly.'

'Then ye'd be better goin' to the pictures,' he growled and slouched off into the crowd.

When the evening came to a close I was singled out by the manager and presented with a large box of chocolates. 'Come back,' he smiled. 'But next time don't sit around on your backside all night. Show them all up! Do the wheelchair twist or something.'

I promised I would, but knew I wouldn't go back. The evening had been an experience, but I needed something in which I could take an active part and I knew I would never find that in a dance hall.

Good times were round the corner for me, but something happened in our lives that put everything else in the background for a time.

Da was taking more and more to his bed. He was neglected and lonely. It was beyond my powers to take meals to his room, so if no one else was at home he had to wait for them. Now nearly eighty-five, his senses were as keen as they had always been, but since Mam's death his morale had been low. We went up to see him but found little to say. We couldn't bridge the gap that had always existed between him and us, but it was easy to be gentle with him. Our fear of him had long gone, though there were times of unease when he went into a temper, his one eye blazing with fury, his large gnarled hands bunched into white, taut knuckles.

His room was reminiscent of the Govan house, with the leering pictures hanging self-consciously on the clean modern walls and smells of apples and tobacco escaping from the drawer in his old-fashioned dresser. The odour of stale smoke clung to his bedclothes, for he still smoked, though in moderation because it gave him the 'water brash'. Away from his watchful eye we were able to have friends in and play records on Kirsty's record player, but we could never be quite certain of his reactions because he was still capable of a few surprises. Sometimes he banged loudly on the floor with his chamber-pot or a shoe – whichever came to hand first; at other times he roared from the top of the stairs, demanding silence. One night he surpassed himself, giving our friends something to remember for the rest of their lives. The records were on and we didn't hear him creeping downstairs. None of us even heard the door opening. 'Turn that bloody juke-box off!' His voice soared in ear-splitting grandeur above the general din. He stood there, a ghastly apparition in his tight-legged, sagging-bottomed combinations. Because he spent so much time in bed, he no longer bothered to wear the glass eye that had once been his pride, and the effect of one solitary eye blazing its fury upon the gathering was not something to be forgotten by the uninitiated.

Margaret's giggly friend stared open-mouthed, Kirsty's latest young man turned white but got up respectfully and turned off the record player. I was fortunate that my friend was a girl who lived next door. She often popped into the house and was used to Da and his ways so I was saved the awful embarrassment that my sisters were showing with their crimson faces.

'Go back to bed, Da,' said Kirsty quietly, 'you'll catch cold.'

'And you'll catch a skelp on the lug if ye don't make less din! This is *my* house!' he cried. There was a look about him, a defeated crushed look. I had never seen it before. His age had caught up with him. He turned slowly and retreated upstairs. I felt an affection for him and a sympathy. How awful to be so old, to have no one to talk to, to spend the long nights alone and to waken up next day with nothing to look forward to but more loneliness.

It was his last grand finale. Several nights later I went to bed early to read a book. I heard Kirsty coming upstairs, going towards Da's room to take him his nightly cup of tea and a biscuit. There was a few moments' silence, then her anguished cry split the night apart. 'Chris! Margaret! Da's dead! Da's dead!'

I don't remember getting into my chair but all at once I was racing through to the adjoining room where Kirsty had crumpled into a chair, her face void of colour. 'Da's dead,' she repeated dazedly. 'I thought he was sleeping and shook him . . . he just . . . fell to the side.'

I looked at my father and saw bubbles of air frothing in his throat, the air of his life expelling itself forever. Quietly he had slipped off on his last journey, his innermost thoughts unknown to us. There was a certain dignity about his going. He had made no fuss, no struggle to hold on to a life that had become empty and meaningless to him.

Once again funeral arrangements had to be made. Again the house was quiet and dark with the scent of flowers hanging heavy in the air. Only fourteen months had lapsed since Mam had been laid to rest. Da hadn't cried then and we had felt bitter towards him. The same old Da, never showing emotions because to him it was weak to display them to the world. The months had gone by and still his eyes remained dry, but gradually we came to realize we had been lucky in finding a release for our grief. His pain had been locked inside and he had simply pined to death.

His coffin was borne away and we all said goodbye to the tough old man who had been our father. Once upon a time we had feared him, but his advancing years and our growing up had lessened our fear and deepened our respect for him. He had commanded respect from everyone who knew him and had received it from many during his long life.

Quite unexpectedly I remembered the toast he had given us every New Year without fail. The memory brought to mind the years of childhood spent in the lofty tenements in Govan. Despite many things they had been good years, filled with all the ingredients that were necessary for a close-knit family circle. There had been a cosiness, too, about our room and kitchen that, no matter how hard we tried to convince ourselves, was undoubtedly missing in the rather cold atmosphere of the new house, where the walls were thin enough to allow neighbours' voices to be heard, neighbours who had come from much the same environment as we had and who went about looking slightly lost without the closes and the landings where a good 'stair-heid' gossip could be enjoyed and where you couldn't help but bump into a well-kent figure every time you went out.

Remembering the years with our parents, I experienced a terrible yearning for the past. So many things belonged to it, Govan, Mam, now Da. One thought gave me comfort. I had come through many years of pain, of turbulent emotions I'd had to suppress. Half of my childhood had gone by in doubt, fear and inactivity. That part of the past I wasn't sorry to let go of, and my mind zoomed away from it quickly.

The funeral cars were going away, a soft August rain was falling, the clouds wept for an old soldier on his final journey.

'Goodbye, Da,' I whispered. 'You don't need the pennies or the whisky now, but you need the heaven and I hope you get it.'

Days to Come

One girl I'd known all through Guides got a little buggy soon after me and we began going everywhere together. We had heard about a club in town for disabled people and to this establishment we took ourselves one evening.

When we arrived at the brightly lit building, I sat hesitating in Bertha but Marie came up to me impatiently, 'Out,' she ordered. 'You'll never get anywhere sitting thinking about it.'

Although Marie had been disabled since infancy with brittle bones, she was quite active. She was small and dark with a rather forceful personality and plenty of confidence. In a way this was good for a born dreamer like me, with very little confidence in myself.

I heaved my chair outside and unfolded it. 'All right,' I answered without enthusiasm. 'But you stay beside me till I get the hang of things.'

A collection of humans propped up by wheels, crutches and sticks milled busily inside the building.

'C'mon,' Marie urged me further into the depths of the hall where table tennis was in progress, played by two boys in wheelchairs. Little groups cohered everywhere. Curious eyes fell upon us. I gulped and put on my nonchalant look. I was extremely good at this, perhaps too successful because my workmates regularly told me I looked either superior or supercilious. I could have told them that the two meant much the same, but that would have been taken as a sign that I was airing my supposed superiority. For a shy person life can be extremely difficult, because if you show you are shy it's an open invitation for others to take the upper hand. If you try to cover your shyness, then the mask you wear to serve the purpose is entirely misconstrued.

A small, heavily built woman, supported by sticks that kept pace with her short legs, came toddling over. 'Hallo,' she said in a deep boom that rocked the foundations of a person's defences. I had expected her voice to match her size. 'I'm Sadie McCraw. C'mon and meet the girls.'

The 'girls' were twice the age we were, but I had long ago discovered that a person's age was of the least importance. To me, personality and character were the things that mattered. Sadie's 'girls' were full of both, with the addition of a sense of fun such as I had never encountered before. Sadie was full of whimsical humour. Her chuckle bubbled out in great throaty gusts as she related experiences she'd had on public transport in an era when there was no provision of invalid cars.

On one occasion she boarded a crowded bus with standing room only, so Sadie tucked herself into the little recess under the stairs. A blithely whistling conductor parked himself in front of her, his posterior level with her face. When her stop came she tapped him on the bottom, requesting access to the platform. The sight of her small, rotund figure so startled him that he shot out of the bus in such a hurry he collided with several passengers, an argument began, and Sadie made good her escape.

Her second anecdote was even funnier. During a heavy snowfall she waited in the bus shelter till the vehicle came. Over she toddled to wait patiently while the conductor, his back turned on her, adjusted his ticket machine.

'Please,' she ventured timidly. 'Could you help me up?' She was of course asking him to help her ascend the high step on to the platform, but when he saw her standing up to her ankles in the snow his face blanched. He couldn't see her legs because they were so short in comparison to her body, which was of normal proportions. 'Oh, my God!' he blabbered in horror. 'The bus is ower yer legs, hen. Hing on and we'll get an ambulance!'

It had taken a few minutes for Sadie to convince him that she wasn't sitting in the snow with her legs pinned under the bus. He had taken her calm request for help as an exceptional show of bravery in extreme circumstances.

'The poor bloke was like a bloody sheet!' Sadie bellowed mirthfully, 'I felt like calling an ambulance for him! I mind another time I went upstairs for a smoke. When my stop came there was quite a crowd on the stairs in front of me and I was feart I would get crushed so I asked a man down below if he would help me at the bottom because I had bad legs. He couldn't see my legs for people and must have thought I was the normal height. Before ye could blink he had grabbed me by the oxters and we both went whizzing down to meet the platform. He just couldny take my weight! I felt sorry for the poor bugger even though I nearly broke my legs!'

'Remember that time we met the wee drunk man?' broke in a tall fair woman with deep dimples and a way of swinging herself carelessly on crutches. Her name was Nellie and her stories were about the different reactions the general public display towards disability. One night she and Sadie emerged from a club run for the disabled. They went walking to the bus stop, a few more of their cronies bringing up the rear. A drunk man came along. Red-nosed, bleary-eyed, he was in a world of his own, bellowing out a distorted rendering of 'I Belong to Glasgow'. When he saw Sadie and Nellie he stopped in his tracks, clinging to a lamp post for support. Nellie was first to be singled out for his hiccuped question, 'Whit – hic – happened tae you, hen – hic?'

Nellie, who was a polio victim, kept her face straight as she answered, 'Hitler did it . . . wi' one o' his bombs.'

'Aw – that's terrible, hen, that's an awful pity,'

sympathized the little man, an unintentional swing round the lamp post bringing his blurred vision to rest on the others. They had heard Nellie's words and were prepared for the next question that would undoubtedly come from the sozzled gentleman, who was now swinging round the lamp post like a drunken monkey. 'My God! Whit happened tae a' youse?' he blabbered in sagging-mouthed horror.

'Same bomb,' came from a trio of voices shaking with pent-up laughter.

The little gentleman landed with a soft thump on the wet pavement. 'That's terrible . . . aw hell, that's terrible,' he muttered dazedly. 'A' youse folk crippled and maimed because o' Hitler! Somebody ought tae *shoot* the bugger!'

We were still laughing when Nellie launched energetically into her next story, one recent enough to make her eyes glint with anger. She had gone into a tea-room with an able-bodied friend. The waitress had ignored Nellie completely, addressing herself only to the able-bod to the point of asking her what kind of things Nellie usually ate. 'By God, I gave the bitch laldy!' said Nellie vigorously. 'I told her tae get me a coconut so that I could throw it at her silly heid! Was her face no' red! I think she learnt her lesson right enough!'

A big man with red hair was bearing down on our group. I had been watching him swing himself all over the hall, the wheelchair attachment that supported his legs being reminiscent of a battering ram. 'What's all this?' he chuckled wickedly. 'Dirty jokes from Sadie again?'

Sadie raised her comically expressive eyebrows. 'We were waiting for you to tell us some,' she said smartly.

'Aw, Sadie,' he grinned, settling square shoulders back in his chair. 'I thought you were my friend . . . actually – I was hoping for an introduction to the new girls,' he finished, flashing me a look from his twinkling brown eyes. Before the night was over Marie and I had promised to accompany him on a buggy run. 'I'll show you how to drive properly!' he roared cheekily as we departed into the night. Bobby Meredith was almost fifteen years older than me but it was the start of the age-old chase between male and female. I wanted no more than a platonic friendship, but soon learned that this was one of the most impossible relationships between the sexes. We argued, laughed, and fought. I kept on running, he kept on pursuing, and we had a whole lot of fun. My social life was now very full and I was out almost every night, greedy for all the good times I had missed in my early teenage years. Often the family were in bed when I came home, and I had good reason to be thankful for all the methods I had devised to overcome obstacles, particularly the one for conquering stairs. Those nearest to me had become so used to my independence that they seldom came to my aid now for anything, which did annoy me sometimes because often a helping hand wouldn't have gone amiss. But sadly, since our parents had gone from our lives, we had all become rather intolerant of each other. Because of my circumstances my life took different paths from the so-called norm which perhaps estranged me slightly from my own kin. The young are often blind to each other's feelings because their vision is so filled with feelings for themselves. No effort is made to analyse each other's thoughts and fears, no questions asked. So it was with us then, and I was glad that Mam had never coddled me in childhood. Otherwise I would never have managed in a house where it was survival of the fittest.

So each night I came home, surmounted the two steps at the porch by sitting on a brick flower box, folding my chair and getting into it, then going through the whole procedure again once inside the house but on a much tougher scale, because of the flight of stairs up to my bedroom. My bottom became hard, my arms strong, and I thanked God for giving me so many different kinds of strength.

Despite my busy life, I was able to rouse myself each morning for work. I was now a reasonably competent machinist and though I didn't enjoy the job I made the best of it, releasing my creative impulses into a little garden I cultivated out of a piece of waste ground in the back yard.

Everyone laughed when I first voiced my ideas.

'Ach, you're daft,' said Lizzie. 'You'd need a tractor tae get rid of these weeds.'

'You wait,' I told her with assurance.

The boss grinned dryly when I put my request to him. 'What's the matter? Aren't you getting enough work in the factory?'

'Plenty,' I hastened to assure him. 'It would just be nicer to sit outside at dinner-time surrounded by flowers.'

My optimism incurred another dry smile, but he gave me the go-ahead for my garden. Armed with a shovel from home and a few feminine wiles, I soon persuaded one of the boys to dig over the ground. After that I raked, hoed and raked, till the earth was nicely brown and free from weeds. Old Gabby the foreman shook his head when he saw me kneeling on my hands and knees with my backside sticking up in the air. 'You're an awfy lassie,' he told me for the umpteenth time. 'You'll never get flowers tae grow there.'

Ignoring all the pessimism, I planted neat rows of seeds, each lunch-time racing outside to peer at the earth for signs of life.

'D'you need a magnifying glass?' asked Lizzie sarcastically.

By June I had an abundance of blooms in my tiny garden. My rose bushes were ebullient with life and I rather hoped the estate gardener wouldn't see them because I had foraged them out of his compost heap.

The boss came out to inspect my handiwork, bringing one of the directors.

'Good show,' said the latter, with the aloof smile

that people of his standing keep for underlings. 'You might come and tidy up my garden a bit, eh?'

I smiled with deceptive charm. 'At five pounds an hour I think you'd find me too expensive.'

He paused, at a loss for words. It certainly wasn't the answer he expected from an employee.

'Oh . . . aha . . . ha – yes, very good,' he mumbled and turned away, my boss making appeasing sounds in his ear.

Lizzie looked at me in amazement. 'You're helluva cocky! Ye wouldny say boo tae a goose a few weeks ago.'

'I had good teachers, Lizzie,' I answered quietly. 'Anyway, why should I lick that old geezer's boots? I hate people who speak down to me.'

Now I was able to pick a large bunch of flowers from my very own garden to take to Mam's grave. I don't know what compelled me to go to the cemetery, because I didn't like to look upon the rows of cold stones. I didn't think of Mam as lying in the crumbling earth, but pictured her in some wonderful place far beyond our planet. The words on her stone were so conventional and meant little to me. What did they tell of her life? There was no indication of the gentle life that had existed between the dates of birth and death. When I left the quiet, dreaming cemetery, it wasn't with the feeling that I was leaving her behind but that she came with me and watched over me, surely the most devoted of guardian angels.

At this time my home life was almost non-existent. The house had no harmony as in days gone by. It was just a place to rest and feed the body. Our views on home management differed greatly, but somehow we kept things ticking over, saw to bills and other unsavoury but necessary items.

There was nothing to keep us together, no head of the house to dictate a routine. Kirsty tried to maintain the family atmosphere, but we resented it if she became too overbearing. She was now going steady with the young man who had made his first encounter with Da under such embarrassing circumstances. We all liked him. He was full of interesting chatter about his upbringing on the Hebridean island of Tiree. After a spell in the Merchant Navy he was now a driver on the Corporation buses with Kirsty as his conductress.

They were married in the spring following Da's death, and the marriage bound the home together after an initial spell of resentment felt by the rest of us. It was strange to watch another man take over Da's role as head of the house. Alec sulked more than any of us, though he had often rebelled against Da's strict regime. But in time we adjusted to the new way of life. I was glad to see Kirsty so happy. She had taken a lot of the responsibilities on her shoulders. Now there was someone to share the load and her whole demeanour became more relaxed.

I never gave a thought to my own future, whether I would get married or not. I lived for each moment.

My wheelchair never got between me and the opposite sex. I had discovered that men more than women accepted you for what you were without too many questions. It wasn't unusual for me to have dates with several partners in one week, places of rendezvous clearer in my mind than the identity of the poor male. Some I liked very much, falling in and out of love so often that Marie was heartily sick of hearing declarations of affection that were as lasting as a puff of wind.

The grass on the other side is always greener. Even while I was going quite steadily with one boy I sighed for the attentions of one young man who was an associate member of our club, which meant that he had all his faculties. He was there to help in the general running of things and was forever rushing to and fro. He was quiet and shy. Sometimes I got a smile from him as he raced past, and I liked the warmth in his blue eyes and his shining thatch of red-gold hair that matched a neat little moustache.

'He's nice,' I remarked to Marie as I watched his slim, agile body flying out of sight.

She sighed impatiently. 'Here we go again! Another lifetime passion that will fade out next week.'

'Do you know his name?' I asked carelessly.

'Everyone just calls him KC. He's always with the older crowd.'

'He must be shy like me,' I decided in a sorrowing voice. 'Sometimes it's easier to get on with older people when you're shy.'

It was June 1962 and our club was busy preparing for the annual rally that was held every year in a playing field outside Glasgow.

The day dawned and scores of bright blue buggies met at an appointed place in town. Excitement was rife when a police car and AA patrolmen on motor bikes arrived to escort us through Glasgow. It was a journey to be remembered because of the gaping pedestrians. Police held up other traffic at the lights, allowing us to sail across like VIPs. My face was crimson with suppressed laughter. Royalty could hardly have looked so important as the long crocodile of invalid cars buzzing noisily along the roads.

At the field everything was chaotic for a time till gradually everyone got sorted into position for the different events. I had put my name down for one or two tests of skill and I manoeuvred myself for Round the Flags, gulping with nerves and telling myself what a fool I was to think I was good enough to compete with people who had been driving for years. Marie had had the good sense not to participate and she waved to me happily from the rows of spectators.

I managed to get round the course without flattening a single flag but my Parking and Garaging was a disaster and I was dryly asked by a steward if I was used to keeping Bertha in a hangar.

Judging the Distance came next and I instructed the stewards to put the posts ever closer till they looked at each other despairingly, a look that said only a female would attempt anything so obviously impossible. But I squeezed through by a hair's breadth, then left the scene with a sigh of relief.

Now that the heats were over I was able to relax and joined Marie to poke round the various stalls. I kept one eye open for KC who was diving about in the distance. He was the Events Convener, which meant that he allotted the stewards their jobs and made sure everything went off smoothly.

'I wish I could talk to him,' I said to Marie, but her answer was drowned in a gay bedlam of sound as the Boys' Brigade struck up on the bagpipes. 'Let's go in for a cuppa!' yelled Marie, and we made our way inside a huge marquee where teacups chinked unceasingly and the butter on homemade pancakes melted in the heat.

I was biting into a large cream doughnut when KC's bright head popped round the marquee doors. 'Christine Fraser!' he called and looked straight at me. 'Your name's being called over the loudspeaker. Could you come at once?'

He disappeared and I was covered in confusion. 'He saw my face!' I told Marie in dismay. 'All covered in cream!'

'Don't be silly, it's only a wee bit on your nose.'

We made our way into the sun. 'How did he know who I was?' I said wonderingly. 'And why is my name being called?'

She clicked her tongue in exasperation. 'I don't know

to the first and you'd better go and find out to the second.'

I was stunned when I was presented with a chrome milk-jug and sugar-bowl, the first prize for Judging the Distance.

'Imagine,' I said dazedly to Marie, 'me winning a prize! How did I do it?'

'I'll never know but congratulations anyway. Now, let's get going.'

We got into our buggies to drive to Marie's house, where I was to have tea before going on to a party. Before leaving the field I looked back and singled out KC who was still rushing about, his bright head shining under the vast expanse of clear blue sky. For a moment the scene was a lovely tableau, the green fields, all that beautiful sky with no chimneys anywhere to mar the effect of space . . . and KC, a young man whose name I didn't even know but who did things to my heart I had never experienced before. I wished that I was staying there among the green fields. With the crowd thinning I might have snatched a chance to talk to him. I knew little about him except that he was an art student in his final year at the Glasgow School of Art.

I wondered again how he had linked my name with my face, but his knowledge of my identity had been no accident, as I was to find out in days to come . . . In days to come! What did they hold for me? How would I overcome the obstacles that would undoubtedly arise for a nineteen-year-old girl, already bereft of both parents and destined to spend the rest of life in a wheelchair?

Marie hooted her horn impatiently and I turned Bertha's snout on to the dusty road, my thoughts surging forward to the night of fun that lay ahead. At that moment nothing really mattered but the present. Nevertheless I looked back again at that elusive figure in the distance. I was living for the present but at that moment I was looking back at my future.

read more

JEFF PEARCE

A POCKETFUL OF HOLES AND DREAMS

The poor boy who made his fortune . . . not just once but twice.

Little Jeff Pearce grew up in a post-war Liverpool slum. His father lived the life of an affluent gentleman whilst his mother was forced to steal bread to feed her starving children. Life was tough and from the moment Jeff could walk he learned to go door to door, begging rags from the rich, which he sold down the markets. Leaving school at the age of fourteen, he embarked on an extraordinary journey, and found himself, before the age of thirty, a millionaire.

Then, after a cruel twist of fate left him penniless, he, his wife and children were forced out of their beautiful home.

With nothing but holes in his pockets, Jeff had no alternative but to go back down the markets and start all over again. Did he still have what it took? Could he really get back everything he had lost?

A Pocketful of Holes and Dreams is the heartwarming true story of a little boy who had nothing but gained everything and proof that, sometimes, rags can be turned into riches . . .

ANGIE BEASLEY

THE FROG PRINCESS

From ugly duckling to beauty queen, this is the touching true tale of how a girl from Grimsby reached the stars.

Life didn't hold much promise for ordinary little Angie. With few jobs around, bland food and cold weather, the best that Angie could hope for was a job at the local Findus factory.

Her family didn't have it easy. Her baby brother was a cot death and the tragedy caused her mother to turn to the Jehovah's Witness faith. Their poverty, now combined with an austere belief system, meant no Christmas, no birthdays and little joy.

But aged 16, Angie decided that she was destined for bigger things. After seeing a TV advertisement she entered a beauty pageant. And won. She went on to take 25 titles, including Miss Leeds, and her home town title Miss Cleethorpes, giving her the opportunity to model while travelling the world.

Just as Angie felt that life couldn't get any better, she got engaged to a man who trapped her in a terrifying cycle of domestic violence. When she eventually escaped him, she had lost all of her money and self-esteem. She was on the bottom rung of the ladder yet again. But Angie picked herself up, turned her talents to event management and grafted her way to becoming Director of Miss England.

Evoking the magical, lost world of the 1970s beauty pageant, Angie's story is a real life fairytale with heart and humour.

MOLLY WEIR

SHOES WERE FOR SUNDAY

'Poverty is a very exacting teacher and I had been taught well'

The post-war urban jungle of the Glasgow tenements was the setting for Molly Weir's childhood. From sharing a pull-out bed in her mother's tiny kitchen to running in terror from the fever van, it was an upbringing that was cemented in hardship. Hunger, cold and sickness was an everyday reality and complaining was not an option.

Despite the crippling poverty, there was a vivacity to the tenements that kept spirits high. Whether Molly was brushing the hair of her wizened neighbour Mrs MacKay, running to Jimmy's chip shop for a ha'penny of crimps or dancing at the annual fair, there wasn't a moment to spare for self-pity. Molly never let it get her down as she and the other urchins knew how to make do with nothing.

And at the centre of her world was her fearsome but loving Grannie, whose tough, independent spirit taught Molly to rise above her pitiful surroundings and achieve her dreams.